Closeness at a Distance:
Leading Virtual Groups to High Performance

Closeness at a Distance: Leading Virtual Groups to High Performance

Dr. Marcus Hildebrandt, Line Jehle, and
Stefan Meister with Susanne Skoruppa

First published in 2013 by Libri Publishing

Copyright © Dr. Marcus Hildebrandt, Line Jehle and Stefan Meister

Authors retain copyright of individual chapters.

The right of Dr. Marcus Hildebrandt, Line Jehle and Stefan Meister to be identified as the authors of this work has been asserted in accordance with the Copyright, Designs and Patents Act, 1988.

ISBN 978 1 909818 00 2
A CIP catalogue record for this book is available from The British Library

Cover design by Helen Taylor

Design by Carnegie Publishing

Libri Publishing
Brunel House
Volunteer Way
Faringdon
Oxfordshire
SN7 7YR

Tel: +44 (0)845 873 3837

www.libripublishing.co.uk

Contents

Foreword   xi

Introduction   1

Chapter One: Our Journey to a Simple Idea: Virtual Closeness
and Purple Spaces   9

Interlude: The Story Begins   35

Chapter Two: Inclusion   39

Chapter Three: Organization and Process   71

Chapter Four: Space and Time   93

Chapter Five: Members, Tasks, and Objectives   121

Chapter Six: E-Culture   149

Interlude: Where Do We Go From Here?   175

Chapter Seven: Selected Aspects of Virtual Leadership   177

Chapter Eight: Media and Technology   201

Chapter Nine: The Virtual Performance Assessment Tool (VPA)
and the Virtual Performance Improvement Process (VPI)   221

Chapter Ten: Case Studies   229

References   257

About the Authors   261

List of Figures, Tables, Text boxes and Exhibits

Figures

Figure 1.1: The Purple Space   19
Figure 1.2: Diversity as a Team Challenge   23
Figure 1.3: Trust and Virtual Closeness   28
Figure 2.1: The Nine Levels of Not Voicing   48
Figure 2.2: Diversity as a Team Challenge   49
Figure 2.3: The Team Clock   54
Figure 4.1: Local Deconstruction   102
Figure 4.2: The Best Time   107
Figure 4.3: Irregular Heartbeat of a Virtual Group   109
Figure 4.4: Group with Team and Network Characteristics   113
Figure 6.1: Online Identity   162
Figure 7.1: The Tolerance Traffic Light   182
Figure 8.1: Divergent and Convergent Communication Processes   203
Figure 8.2: Synchronous and Asynchronous Media in
Convergent and Divergent Communication Processes   205
Figure 8.3: Interaction Spaces: Examples   207
Figure 8.4: Regular Heartbeat of a Virtual Group   209
Figure 8.5: Irregular Heartbeat of a Virtual Group   210
Figure 8.6: Maturity Levels of Virtualization   212
Figure 8.7: The Team Clock   217
Figure 10.1: 4-Step Program for Virtual Team Development   232
Figure 10.2: Selected Results of the Virtual Performance
Assessment of the Global Team   235
Figure 10.3: Selected Results of the Virtual Performance
Assessment of the UK Group   235

Tables

Table 1.1: The Difference between Collocated and Virtual
Team Development   10
Table 1.2: Challenges and Opportunities of Remote Collaboration 13
Table 2.1: Shared Leadership Scenarios   62, 63
Table 8.1: Purpose, Media, and Synchronicity   206
Table 8.2: Media and Purpose   206

Textboxes

Textbox 1.1: Working Together: Teams, Groups, or Networks?   11
Textbox 1.2: Three Rules for Successful Virtual Collaboration   21
Textbox 1.3: VPA Categories   31
Textbox 2.1: Definition: Dimension "Feedback Competence"   47
Textbox 2.2: Definition: Dimension "Communication Styles"   51
Textbox 2.3: Example: Communication and Pause Patterns   52
Textbox 2.4: Definition: Dimension "Work Styles"   56
Textbox 2.5: Work Styles: Typical Questions and Possible
Answers   59
Textbox 2.6: Definition: Dimension "Shared Leadership"   60
Textbox 3.1: Definition: Dimension "Access to Information and
Power"   76
Textbox 3.2: Definition: Dimension "Workflow Integration"   79
Textbox 3.3: Definition: Dimension "Organizational Relevance"   81
Textbox 3.4: Definition: Dimension "Self-Organization Skills"   84
Textbox 4.1: Definition: Dimension "Geographic Advantage"   100
Textbox 4.2: Definition: Dimension "Work Schedule Overlap"   103
Textbox 4.3: Definition: Dimension "Time Shared in Dialogue"   108
Textbox 4.4: Definition: Dimension "Time Investment"   112
Textbox 5.1: Definition: Dimension "Language Skills"   126
Textbox 5.2: Do You Speak Globish?   128
Textbox 5.3: Definition: Dimension "Quality of Relationships"   130
Textbox 5.4: Definition: Dimension "Information Sharing"   133
Textbox 5.5: Definition: Dimension "Identification with Group
and Objectives"   138
Textbox 6.1: Definition: Dimension "Virtual Experiences"   153
Textbox 6.2: Definition: Dimension "Global Netiquette Skills"   156
Textbox 6.3: Definition: Dimension "Media Competence"   158

Textbox 6.4: Definition: Dimension "Online Identity
Competence" 161
Textbox 6.5: Creating Social Presence in a Phone Conference 164
Textbox 6.6: Indicators for Cognitive Presence 165
Textbox 6.7: Indicators for Leadership Presence 166
Textbox 7.1: Steps in Deep Democracy Negotiations 188
Textbox 7.2: Guidelines for Mediating Virtual Leadership 194, 195
Textbox 9.1: Orientation Questions 225
Textbox 9.2: Note 226
Textbox 10.1: Key Takeaways 243

Exhibits

Exhibit 9.1: VPA Output Example 223
Exhibit 10.1: Workshop Agenda 233
Exhibit 10.2: Workshop Agenda (Step 3) 236, 237
Exhibit 10.3: Outcomes 238
Exhibit 10.4: Content Container 238
Exhibit 10.5: Reflecting VPA Results 239
Exhibit 10.6: Strengths of the team 240
Exhibit 10.7: Brainstorming: Media Mix 241

Acknowledgments

This book was realized through virtual teamwork, interspersed with some face-to-face sessions. We are deeply grateful to all those people whose support and contributions encouraged us and made this project an extraordinary experience.

We wish to thank Jessica Lipnack and Karen Sobel Lojesky. Without their pioneering research this work would not have been possible. We are grateful to our customers and workshop participants from whom we were able to learn so much of the knowledge conveyed in this book. We would like to thank eBay and RWE in particular for allowing us to include case studies from our work with them. We also thank our colleagues in the organizational consulting arena for inspiring partnerships and exchanges.

Special thanks go to Andrea Mendieta, Josephina Görlach, Chen Wang, Menakai Yogachelvam, Malii Brown, Rebecca Friese, and Sumaiah El-Said of the intercultures team who provided invaluable research support and comments. We also thank Anette Grimmelsmann and Sujata Banerjee for very helpful comments and suggestions.

We acknowledge and thank the team at Libri Publishing for their patience and guidance.

Line Jehle wishes to thank Frank Jehle for his extensive and invaluable comments on the manuscript.

Finally, we express our deepest gratitude to our partners and families for their patience and the time they granted us away from them to invest in this book.

The authors
Berlin, November 2013

Foreword

In 1998, Jeff Stamps and I received a request from a reader of our book, *Virtual Teams*. If you write enough books, it isn't unusual to hear from enthusiastic readers. Over the years, we've received many emails, calls, and even, if you can remember back that far, letters. But this one was different. Marcus Hildebrandt, a consultant in Germany, was asking to visit. Although the book had been published in German, he'd read it in English and was so taken with the content that he wanted to meet with us face to face.

And so he did. Of course, we were very touched that someone would travel across an ocean to meet. We had a good conversation, told him a bit about ourselves, and vice-versa, the kind of meeting that is good for both parties. And life went on. Every few years, Marcus would drop a note about something he was doing in regard to virtual teams and, when a request came in from Germany, I'd often refer the person to him.

Then in December of 2012 came another note from Marcus, subject line: "Long time no read – good news!" With flattering words about our work still having an effect on him, Marcus brought me up to date. He'd been working with a team of consultants, including Stefan Meister and Line Jehle, and together they'd written a new book on virtual teams.

While I trusted that anything Marcus was involved with would be good, frankly I didn't think the world needed another book on virtual teams. Since ours, which was likely the first – it's dangerous to claim absolutism in regard to being the first at anything since someone somewhere probably beat you to it and you simply don't know it – there have been dozens. Indeed, we've been asked to write the forewords to a number of them. Generally speaking, these are good books but, after so many have been written, it's very difficult to find something original. Just search the topic and you'll see what I mean. In my opinion, many are derivative, repetitive, and not terribly inspired, "cut-and-paste" jobs that take face-to-face ideas and attempt to bolt them onto the virtual world. It doesn't work.

Then came a video conference where I met Marcus's collaborators and, in the course of that conversation, I came to understand that this savvy group had innovative approaches and a lot of energy, intelligence, and compassion, all key to virtual working. They also were comfortable talking about the death in 2011 of my co-author and collaborator of decades, Jeff Stamps. Empathic human beings rise to the level of minor deities in my hierarchy of positive traits. Before the call was over, I was so taken with their new approaches that I offered to write this Foreword.

A few months later, Stefan and Marcus came to visit. We spent a day and an evening together, talking about what we were interested in, telling one another our life stories. In the course of the day, the title of the book came up and suddenly a new one emerged, "Closeness at a Distance." The phrase described what we were experiencing and what must happen for virtual groups to work well together.

Reading this book was a delight. There are so many new ideas here – from references to interesting developments like the Virtual Choir, where people from around the world join voices online, to very practical ideas like giving feedback in structured and productive ways.

While reading, I made a list of the ideas that were new to me: the German word *Zuverlässigkeit* means "you can leave me with it," which is key to collaboration; that it's critical to create "Purple Space," where virtual working can take root and bloom; that a virtual group flourishes within "a culture of flowing feedback;" that it's important to "hunt for the 'No'" spread it, and "ask how you can help;" that the "Thai know more than a dozen different ways to smile only a few of which are recognizable to Western perception;" and that "one of the most frequent assessments of US American smiles from a German perspective is that they are fake".

Zounds. And that's just the start.

I'm certain that when you read this book you'll be making margin notes galore (or digital comments, as I did), and will find yourself far better equipped to experience *Closeness at a Distance.*

Jessica Lipnack, author of *Virtual Teams* and *The Age of the Network*
West Newton, Massachusetts, USA
September 2013

Introduction

Who This Book Is For * Your Benefit of Reading This Book * How This Book Is Structured * Improving Virtual Performance by Creating Virtual Closeness * Collaboration 3.0: Creating *"Purple Spaces"* * Measuring Virtual Closeness: The Virtual Performance Assessment (VPA)

Who This Book Is For

This book is written for all those who are involved in virtual collaboration and seek to reach levels of high performance. Leaders and managers as well as members of virtual teams, groups, and networks[*] will profit from the approach detailed in this book as much as consultants, coaches, and trainers.

Your Benefit of Reading This Book

After reading this book you will know a structured approach to leading virtual groups to high performance.

---

[*] Throughout the book, we will use "groups" to refer to teams, groups, and networks.

How This Book Is Structured

This book is divided into three parts:

Part One

The first part (chapters One to Six) focuses on Virtual Closeness and Purple Spaces. The reader is then introduced to the five categories through which the twenty dimensions of Virtual Closeness are operationalised: Inclusion; Organization and Process; Space and Time; Members, Tasks, and Objectives; and E-Culture. To illustrate these categories, each chapter is preceded by a corresponding section of a fictitious story about a global virtual team led by Florian Bell, a German manager from Munich.

Part Two

In the second part (chapters Seven and Eight), we discuss selected aspects of virtual leadership and the role of media and technology in virtual collaboration. This part is slightly more theoretical than Part One and can be referred to for specific questions in these two areas. Given that the choice and implementation of media use is a leadership task, the second half of Chapter Eight will be of particular interest to those leading or consulting virtual groups.

Part Three

The third part will be of particular use to consultants applying VPA (Virtual Performance Assessment) ® and VPI (Virtual Performance Improvement) ® to their global virtual clients' needs. VPA and VPI, as well as their various application scenarios, are explained (Chapter Nine). We then present four case studies from our work with different clients (Chapter Ten). They show customized VPI processes based on the clients' VPA results and subsequent diagnostic work.

Improving Virtual Performance by Creating Virtual Closeness

After working with virtual groups for more than a decade, we felt we were, in a modest way, successful in our efforts; but we would nevertheless hit limits. This often happened in two areas:

- The clients' realities were growing so complex that they often required half a day or more of precious face-to-face time to understand and map out their processes and networks.

- Even when we had succeeded in disentangling their landscapes of collaboration, clients often wanted everything at once from a workshop and it was thus hard to satisfy all their demands.

In short, we had the feeling we were lacking precision in face of increasing complexity. As these experiences were accumulating, we decided it was time to do something about it. For two years we researched and evaluated our own experiences and also those of others, drawing from contact with and learning from the pioneers in the field: Jessica Lipnack, Jeffrey Stamps, and Karen Sobel Lojesky.

Our breakthrough came when we realized that there was indeed one unifying success criteria for all virtual teams, groups, and networks: the degree of perceived "closeness" felt towards the group, the project/process, the stakeholders, and/or the organization involved – ***Virtual Closeness***. Virtual Closeness lies at the core of our approach to working with virtual groups.

> **Virtual Closeness describes the perceived closeness between two or more group members and their perceived closeness to the context and space wherein they interact (what we chose to call *"Purple Space"*) after a period of little or no face-to-face contact.**

What makes the concept of Virtual Closeness unique is that it doesn't only refer to people feeling close to each other. It also implies that people feel close to the spaces wherein they communicate and collaborate and to the mental objects that represent the virtual work environment such as processes and structures. This understanding of closeness is crucial in late modernity when globalization and advanced technology have created new and rather intangible virtual interaction spaces. Especially in business environments, these virtual spaces – as a critical success factor for high performance – need to be even more attractive than the virtual spaces that are visited outside of working time. Taking care of the building blocks of Virtual Closeness helps virtual groups to create a unique and shared identity and a feeling of belonging and immersion in these spaces and the organization wherein the space is embedded.

Collaboration 3.0: Creating *"Purple Spaces"*

The second central innovative concept we are introducing in this book is that of **Purple Space**. Purple Space denotes an advanced level of maturity in working virtually, which is achieved through the reduction of complexity of that new interaction space in which groups meet and collaborate. Group members usually already belong to a local interaction space encompassing elements such as a local working and communication culture; local rules, processes, and organizational structures; local technology; and local people, to whom they might feel more or less close. One member may join from a "blue" space, another from a "red" space. Consider a German manager who is part of a global team. He works from his local "blue" space (or any other colour) and is used to making preferably "blue" decisions that benefit his local community. Overall growth, however, happens when organizations create an additional new space of belonging in which people feel close to each other and start taking responsibility on a more global scale, thereby creating benefits for the whole group, project and/or organization instead of only its respective local members. In our example, the organization will thrive once the German manager starts to facilitate "purple" choices and decisions that benefit the entire group ("blue" and "red") rather than only his local organizational interests.

Purple Space is a collaboration space that is intentionally created for the purpose of allowing the virtual collaboration of a group. It is characterized by a certain degree of frictionless communication and collaboration processes in a global environment and is thus an artificial social innovation that has to be built for its specific purpose. The currency of the Euro as represented on the coins (not necessarily as a monetary construct) was, when introduced, a fitting example of a Purple Space. One side of the coin represented the old identity (e.g. the king of Spain, the German eagle – equivalent to our blue, yellow, green, and red spaces etc.) while the other side represented a new, common one (purple). In creating the Purple Space, the other spaces also became better known to each other, just as a Euro from France can arrive in an Austrian wallet. Reviewing history, we can also determine that a currency is a construct closely linked to the identities of people and, as such, it is not easily given up. In the case of the Euro, users gained not only an additional identity (purple) but also deeper knowledge about the other identities – including, potentially, their own.

Purple Spaces are partly negotiated by all group members. The members can shift between purple and local spaces depending on the task. A Purple Space is designed to allow users to build a shared identity for their work in virtuality. By building on diversity rather than standardizing it, this fosters performance by drawing from the benefits of having different approaches to working together, to fulfilling tasks, and to solving conflicts.

Think of Purple Space as a "glocal" construct – the marriage of multiple local identities to create a global one. In virtual collaboration, group members can be present both in their local and global spaces as demanded by the project and their organizations. The local spaces continue to exist and a new – *purple* – space is added for the specific purpose of global virtual collaboration.

The concepts of Virtual Closeness and Purple Space are intimately interconnected. A new common identity can be much more easily created in a Purple Space if members feel virtually close. A shared identity is the precondition for achieving high performance. To illustrate what we mean, consider the principle of attractiveness. In order for someone truly to want to engage in a project, the circumstances need to be attractive enough for them to commit their time and energy. In virtual collaboration, the virtual space wherein participants meet needs to have that measure of attractiveness. Further, only when bound with Virtual Closeness will people cooperate efficiently in Purple Spaces.

Measuring Virtual Closeness: The Virtual Performance Assessment (VPA)

In order to help groups to create and foster Virtual Closeness and reduce complexity in Purple Spaces, we have developed the VPA (Virtual Performance Assessment) * tool and the VPI (Virtual Performance Improvement) * process. In this book, we explain in detail how VPA works through measuring and developing Virtual Closeness in twenty operational dimensions. And we introduce you to VPI, a holistic group or Organization Development (OD) process, with the help of a case study.

VPA measures the users' perception of Virtual Closeness concerning the status of their virtual collaboration processes, thus producing descriptive, non-judgmental results. These results present a virtual group's tune, its melody as perceived by the individual group members, at a given point in time. This tune can be based on a single melody shared by group members if their perceptions are similar; or it can be a portfolio – or at worst, a cacophony – of melodies if perceptions vary.

The assessment thus maps a framework that shows the "hot spots of Virtual Closeness" of a group's virtual collaboration and identifies specific starting points for interventions.

It is within this framework that the *Virtual Performance Improvement* process is designed and implemented. Following the principle of attractiveness, it builds on a group's strengths in order to improve any existing deficits. A VPI process can be started with a *Virtual Performance Assessment* to elicit the group's tune. VPA is designed in such a way that it can be conducted several times during a team process to record the progress made through targeted interventions to improve performance.

Developed from an Organization Development perspective and as a diagnostic tool, VPA fulfils multiple functions. Apart from being an assessment tool, it also encourages discussion and learning about the twenty dimensions of creating Virtual Closeness and reduces complexity in Purple Spaces. For a virtual group, filling out VPA and discussing the experience encourages building a common identity and the design of a new collaboration space that is best suited for this group or organization: its customized Purple Space. It is therefore simultaneously a first step towards creating Virtual Closeness and the initial building bloc of a Virtual Performance Improvement process.

VPA is a highly practical hands-on tool that has been developed and tested in many years of consulting work and from our own experiences in organizations. The concepts and terminology used are directly derived from everyday organizational contexts. It is also an international tool that has been developed by a cross-cultural team with several decades of experience working and living in different cultures. Encompassing the complexity of virtual collaboration in connecting the specific groups' purpose with technology, leadership, and culture, VPA covers the full complexity teams, groups, or networks face when working together across a distance.

CHAPTER ONE

Our Journey to a Simple Idea: Virtual Closeness and Purple Spaces

1.1   The Two Sides of Working Together Remotely

1.2   Virtual Closeness in Purple Spaces

1.3   Virtual Performance Assessment (VPA) at a Glance

This chapter lays the theoretical groundwork of this book. We are introducing the concepts of Virtual Closeness and Purple Space that underpin the practice of Virtual Performance Improvement.

After mapping out the challenges and opportunities of virtual collaboration, we will trace and define the concept of Virtual Closeness and identify the success factors of working together virtually. Finally, we will delineate Virtual Closeness from the notion of trust.

After reading this chapter, you will understand how we arrived at the notions of Virtual Closeness and Purple Space, what they entail, and how they differ from other concepts about enhancing virtual collaboration.

1.1 The Two Sides of Working Together Remotely: Rethinking Challenges and Identifying Opportunities

Answer the following questions as spontaneously as possible: Do you think it is preferable to work face-to-face or in close physical proximity? Or do you prefer to work virtually? If you choose the first option, you are in the company of a vast majority of people working virtually and internationally.

It is widely believed that groups working together remotely with the help of virtual tools do not perform as well as physically collocated groups. Unfortunately, from our experience we know that this is often true. A number of studies show that, on average, virtual groups tend to perform less effectively than collocated ones. This low performance tends to be magnified even when the virtual group operates across cultural boundaries.

So much for the bad news. The good news is that, given the right tools and under adequate management, virtual groups can perform extremely well. Several studies published during the last decade show that under certain circumstances, remote teams can even outperform collocated ones[1]. An article by Majchrzak, Malhotra, Stamps, and Lipnack, published 2004 in the *Harvard Business Review* and voted one of the top ten articles on building effective teams in 2011, specifies that while remote groups tend to perform more poorly than collocated groups, those that perform well can actually outperform collocated groups[2]! This signifies an enormous opportunity for creating high-performance virtual groups.

Table 1.1: The Difference between Collocated and Virtual Team Development

Collocated Teams	Virtual Teams
Synchronous team development:	Asynchronous team development:
Members go through all team phases (forming, norming, storming, etc.) at the same time	Members are disconnected in space and time and may perceive themselves to be in different team phases

We have been consulting a large number of managers who work in remote settings as part of virtual groups. While they usually grow into their role of managing virtually, many of those leaders admit to finding the task difficult when asked about their experience. In the German-speaking countries, for example, two-thirds of virtual leaders do not perceive themselves as being successful at managing remotely[3]. The reasons managers typically offer also point out the differences between managing collocated and virtual groups, including, for example: different locations, time zones, technology, communication, cultural behaviours, and language.

Textbox 1.1: Working Together: Teams, Groups, or Networks?

Throughout the book, you will find the terms "team(s)", "group(s)", and "network(s)". They each delineate overlapping forms of organizing people at work. Teams are set up for a certain period of time and are characterized by common goals towards which members combine their efforts within the broader framework of interdependent tasks. Groups come together for the common purpose of fulfilling a specific task or project for a limited period of time or on a recurring process-related basis. Each group member has her/his own independent task. Most people in global organizations work in both teams and groups.

Teams and groups are embedded in social networks. Networks are more flexible and looser, purposeful settings wherein workers accomplish a task together. Both group and network members usually report to managers outside of the group or network. They are highly flexible, spreading their knowledge and skills across time and space while handling different tasks simultaneously. In most cases, there is a core group or a core team that is responsible for the coordination of the contributions of the network towards a common purpose or goal.

We find that many organizations use the term "team" when they are actually dealing with groups or even networks.

Thus, task-related group and network configurations are particularly common in global, virtual organizations.

To cater to the reality of virtual work, we consistently use "group(s)" to represent teams, groups, or networks throughout this book and our work more broadly, including the Virtual Performance Assessment tool, unless we specifically intend to refer to teams or networks.

In light of such complexity, two questions arise. First, one might ask whether it makes any sense at all to work together virtually. The answer is yes, of course it does. In fact, the question is not very helpful given that virtuality has become indispensable in today's working world. This trend is highly unlikely to be reversed. In the global business environment, where many internationally oriented companies are already operating or will enter in the future, remoteness is an inevitable element of competition.

The second question is whether there are ways to overcome those difficulties; and again, the answer is yes, definitely. Not only can we overcome the intricacies of remote collaboration, but with good virtual leadership we can actually use the benefits of working globally and capitalize on the high diversity found in global groups. Moving attention from difficulties to opportunities also marks a paradigm shift: rather than settling for a virtuality that complicates our work processes, organizations can focus on the strengths of remote collaboration to increase performance significantly.

Think of the strengths of virtual collaboration as treasures hidden underneath the widely perceived difficulties – treasures which are unique to virtual groups and which must be found and cared for. Virtual group success is about redefining differences and difficulties inherent to remote work as a special feature that is absent in collocated teams and groups. In other words, when looked at from a perspective of potential rather than one of lack, remoteness becomes a competitive advantage. Diversity becomes one of the main keys to success.

In the table below, we redefine typical difficulties of working together remotely in the context of high diversity as opportunities.

Table 1.2 (opposite): Challenges and Opportunities of Remote Collaboration

	Challenges	Opportunities
Different locations	Group members are located in different cities, countries, regions, or on other continents, making it difficult to get everyone together at the same time.	When a group is spread across different geographical locations, its members are close to various decision makers throughout the organization and able to draw a much larger influencing radius. Also, group members are close to regional customers, thus offering direct service globally. They can further choose the place they work from which gives them great flexibility and the potential for enhanced work–life balance, thus adding to identification with the group and/or project.
Different time zones	Group members may work across different time zones with seeming incompatibility between day and night working hours.	Due to the time differences, teams can literally be productive around the clock. In a well-functioning group, issues faced by those asleep can be resolved by far-flung colleagues who are awake so that the former may wake to an "overnight" solution. With group members in countries where the working week includes Saturdays and/or Sundays, 24 hours a day can even become 24 hours a day, seven days a week.
Technology	Technological equipment, access to it and/or the quality of connections often differ strongly, thus easily impeding communication.	When different cultural systems grow together, technologies do, too. Group members can now access the same knowledge from different locations, enhancing their media competences and saving significant costs, especially for travel.
Cultural behaviours	People of different cultures tend to solve problems differently or have a differing understanding of when something is completed. This applies to geographies as much as to differing organizational units. Local cultural norms are usually implicit and taken for granted, even in a global context.	When we regard diversity in ideas about work and in ways of solving problems and handling issues not as a barrier or threat but, rather, as a huge potential of creative solutions for a large array of topics, unprecedented opportunities will open up. Perhaps the main benefit of cultural heterogeneity is that no fixed culture exists and groups have to negotiate their own culture – a new culture.

The kind of leadership necessary to redefine weaknesses as strengths and create and manage high-performing groups, however, does not often come naturally. Excellent virtual management skills require training, as do skills required for group members to thrive in a virtual environment. A copy-and-paste approach from a collocated management role does not work in virtual groups. Rather, managing a virtual group requires leaders and members alike to learn and focus on new knowledge and skills in order to fully appreciate and include cultural diversity. Moreover, strong technological competences are key and the younger generations are often leading the way when it comes to acquiring media competences. Also, in complex virtual environments it is almost impossible to keep a constant overview of what is happening in the different participating locations. The ability to "deal with the unknown" in a professional manner is therefore another key competence of virtual leaders. In Chapter Seven, we will discuss in greater detail virtual leadership in the context of Virtual Performance Improvement.

1.2 Virtual Closeness in Purple Spaces: Our Journey to a Simple Idea

While it is difficult for virtual groups to be successful, it is certainly possible. What's more, once virtual collaboration works well and aspects of diversity previously perceived as obstacles are redefined and experienced as strengths, those groups can even outperform collocated ones[4].

So how is this shift from difficulty to opportunity accomplished? How do virtual groups go from poor to high performance?

- Through creating or enhancing Virtual Closeness between their members and between the members and the working context

- and by creating a new space of collaboration – the Purple Space.

Here is how we arrived at this central tenet during many years of working with virtual teams, groups, and networks and conducting targeted research.

Consider our teenage generations. Tech-savvy and mobile, they communicate constantly through text-based messaging services such as SMS, What's App or Facebook. They feel close to each other without being physically close, sometimes living in different countries. In virtuality, they have their own space of belonging. The same is true for online dating. Often, two people exchange large volumes of private information through a structured shared space before they meet. Why? To build trust virtually as the basis for a face-to-face meeting. Another example is receiving a letter from a loved one far away. The act of reading the letter produces a feeling of closeness without physically being near the other. Also, think of the growing number of successful online start-ups that acquire and maintain their clients, and deliver their services, almost entirely through communication in dedicated virtual spaces. Even counseling, coaching, and mediation are now offered over the phone, via Skype, or on websites with individuals most customers have never met physically but whom they trust because of being intimately familiar with their work through ample online interaction in shared virtual spaces.

> ➤ *Example: The Virtual Choir*
> If you have ever been a part of a choir, you have experienced musical connection with others. The senses of the group heighten and the group attunes towards a common sound. In some sense, it seems that a similar phenomenon has now occurred virtually. The so-called Virtual Choir is a symphony of individual audio-visual recordings that are technically synchronized to resemble the sound of a choir; in more ways than one, this is a *virtual* choir. In simulating a real-time, collocated choir, members of the virtual choir achieve closeness in a virtual environment. The first Virtual Choir ("Lux Aurumque", meaning "light and gold") included 185 videos from 12 countries; Virtual Choir 2 ("Sleep") included over 2,000 videos from 60 countries; and most recently, Virtual Choir 3 ("Water Night") boasted 3,746 videos from 73 different countries!
>
> How does the Virtual Choir work? Composer Eric Whitacre, originator of the Virtual Choir, makes an open call and posts an online video of himself "conducting" different sections of the choir. In turn, respondents from around the world submit video recordings of themselves singing to Whitacre's direction. From there,

video technicians and an audio team do their work. Facebook is the shared virtual communication platform for people to interact with one another in relation to the choir. To date, the page has earned over 26,000 "likes". As an example of Virtual Closeness, a virtual community has been born and is flourishing. Virtuality is their concert hall, their space wherein they meet and sing together.

This example shows that an experience of deeply felt closeness can exist independently of geographical proximity. Thanks to media and technology, one can feel close to far-flung others and their shared space of collaboration and its purpose over extended periods of time – as close as when together physically. Relationships and the feeling of belonging can be built virtually.

For this, a sense of equality is key. The members of the choir come together in their online concert hall as equals. This points to a necessary shift in thinking about working together virtually. When joining an online meeting or a phone conference, the notion of someone being brought into the meeting is still widely spread. This presupposes one person, say a manager, who is responsible for bringing her group members into a phone or video conference with far-flung partners. For a collaboration space to work and be filled with closeness – the prerequisites of a Purple Space – however, it is vital that we think of participants as coming together in the common interaction space. The manager (or the organization) provides and partly fills this space with a structure, thereby fulfilling a typical task of virtual leadership. Rather than being brought into the meeting by someone else, they join the Purple Space as equal participants – each and every one of them.

From Virtual Distance to Building Virtual Closeness in a Space of Shared Interaction (Purple Space)

In their pioneering research work about the "virtual workforce", Karen Sobel Lojeski and Richard R. Reilly examined this phenomenon[5]. They conceptualized the lack of the experience of feeling virtually close to others as *virtual distance* and identified three categories of separation: physical distance, operational distance, and affective distance. Distance does not only refer to spatial distance in this context but also encompasses the emotional dimension of feeling separated.

> *Virtual Distance describes the perceived distance between two or more people in communication or cooperation scenarios with little or no face-to-face contacts.*

For organizational performance, Lojesky and Reilly stipulated that virtual success depends on reducing virtual distance in three corresponding areas: culturally, operationally, and organizationally[6].

In applying the concept of virtual distance to our work with customers, however, we soon found that the notions of "reducing" and "distance" have a negative connotation when in fact our goal is to encourage and increase motivation in virtual performance. We therefore developed what we perceive as a more motivational approach: that of Virtual Closeness. The tested underlying assumption holds that the closer groups feel virtually, the better they will perform and the more success they will have.

The other cornerstone of our approach is that of Purple Space. Purple Space is a collaboration space that is intentionally created for the purpose of virtual collaboration of a group.

When people from different parts of the organization and with different professional backgrounds come together in a virtual space, productivity usually drops significantly in face of the many different ways of doing things. These approaches represent the members' local cultures and are therefore usually considered as the "right" way of doing things by them. This propensity for chaos often creates negative feelings in people entering virtual spaces.

To counter and prevent a negative experience, we offer the concept of a Purple Space.

Purple Space is the global interaction space wherein virtual groups can reach high performance.

We chose purple because it denotes a mix of basic colours such as red and blue. These basic colours represent local cultures that feed into a transcultural (purple) dimension.

Purple has differing meanings across cultures. It can represent the spirit and spirituality as well as darker aspects of the psyche. It is the colour of Hinduism and of feminism, but also of mysticism. Aware of these different representations, we associate purple with positive aspects. To us, it symbolizes the transcendent quality of harmonizing contrasts.

Purple Space denotes a certain level of maturity and a reduction of complexity of that new interaction space in which groups meet when working virtually. Group members usually belong to a local interaction space encompassing elements such as a local working and communication culture; local rules, processes, and organizational structures; local technology; and local people. One member may join from a "blue" space, another from a "red" space. Consider a German manager who is part of a global team. He works from his local "blue" space (or any other colour) and is used to make preferably "blue" decisions that benefit his local community. Overall growth, however, happens when organizations create an additional, new space of belonging in which people feel close to each other and start taking responsibility on a more global scale, thereby creating benefits for the whole organization instead of only its respective local members. In our example, the organization will thrive once the German manager starts to make "purple" choices and decisions that benefit the entire group ("blue" and "red") rather than only his local team.

Purple Space is a collaboration space that is intentionally created for the purpose of containing the virtual collaboration of a group. A Purple Space is characterized by a certain degree of frictionless communication and collaboration processes in a global environment and is thus an artificial social innovation that has to be built on purpose. The currency of the Euro was, when introduced, a fitting example of

Figure 1.1: The Purple Space

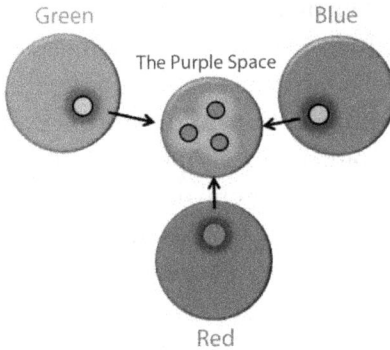

a Purple Space. One side represented the old identity (blue, yellow, green, red, etc.), while the other side represented a new, common one (purple). In creating the Purple Space, the other spaces also became better known to each other, just as a Euro from Spain can arrive in an Austrian wallet. Reviewing history, we can also determine that a currency is a construct closely linked to the identity of people, so it is not easily given up. In the case of the Euro, we did not only gain one additional identity (purple), but also deeper knowledge about the other identities.

Purple Spaces are partly negotiated by all group members. The members can shift between the purple and local spaces depending on the task. A Purple Space is designed to allow users to build a shared identity for their work in virtuality. By building on, rather than standardizing, diversity, it fosters performance by drawing from the benefits of having different approaches to working together, to fulfilling tasks, and to solving conflicts.

Think of Purple Space as a "glocal" construct – the marriage of multiple local identities to create a global one. In virtual collaboration, group members can be present both in their local and global spaces as demanded by the project. The local spaces continue to exist, and a new – purple – space is added for the specific purpose of global virtual collaboration.

The concepts of Virtual Closeness and Purple Space are intimately interconnected. A new common identity can be created in a Purple Space if members feel virtually close. A shared identity is the precondition for achieving high performance. To illustrate what we mean, consider the principle of attractiveness. In order for someone truly to want to engage in a project, the circumstances need to be attractive enough for them to commit their time and energy. In virtual collaboration, the virtual space wherein participants meet needs to have that measure of attractiveness. Further, only when filled with Virtual Closeness will people cooperate efficiently in Purple Spaces.

Based on this understanding, we have developed the following definition of Virtual Closeness and Purple Space:

> *Virtual Closeness describes the perceived closeness between two or more group members and their perceived closeness to the context and space wherein they interact (what we chose to call "Purple Space") after a period of little or no face-to-face contact.*

Success Factors for Virtual Collaboration

To understand the circumstances wherein members of virtual groups feel close, we have been asking our clients for many years about the factors that create and enhance an experience of closeness in virtual collaboration project scenarios. Some exemplary aspects include:

- Identifying with the project and its members
- Putting faith into the project and trusting project members
- Being committed to the project
- Short communication paths
- Being understood by the other members
- Sharing a common identity
- The project being always on one's mind
- Having a clear picture of the project

- Assuming responsibility for the project's success

- Using a shared and frictionless virtual space for the above.

Studying 54 global virtual teams in 26 different companies, Majchrzak et al. found that "absence can make a team grow stronger" and developed three rules for successful virtual collaboration as shown in the following table[7].

Textbox 1.2: Three Rules for Successful Virtual Collaboration

Majchrzak et al. (2004) developed the following three rules for successful virtual collaboration from studying 54 global virtual teams in 26 different companies.

Rule No. 1: Exploit diversity
- Build on the strength of people's differences
- "Storm to form" and don't "form to storm"
- Engage in many in-depth, inclusive conversations
- Allow conversation to change
- Use team evaluations and inform the team members of the scores
- To avoid cliquing, form rotating collaborative pairs of people with different perspectives.

→ Major differences between team members will often lead to break through solutions!

Rule No. 2: Use technology to simulate reality
- Combine telephone conferences (86 per cent) with virtual work spaces (83 per cent)
- Use online threaded discussions during teleconferences and between meetings
- In the research, instant messaging was a preferred mode of communication to voice immediate thoughts and feelings
- Video conferences and email were not preferred modes of team communication in the study.

Rule No. 3: Hold the team together
- Communicate daily and intensively
- Choose/create a common language (for example Portuñol, a hybrid of Spanish and Portuguese adopted by a pan South American Unilever team)
- Integrate the work processes of team members
- Protect team members by agreeing on time concessions with home managers
- Orchestrate telephone conferences as events that no-one would want to miss.

We found that these three rules for successful virtual collaboration can be adapted and paraphrased as success factors for creating and maintaining Virtual Closeness in global, task-oriented groups.

Success factor # 1: Exploiting diversity → Getting closer culturally

This is achieved by using the potential of cultural diversity represented in a group. As discussed earlier, this is not an easy thing to accomplish. A closer look at diversity in groups is therefore in order.

In 2000, Joseph DiStefano and Martha Maznevski[8] described the status quo of research on multicultural teams before they began their own systematic study of these, stating that:

> *"in no research did diverse teams outperform homogenous ones on overall solution quality, and in only one study did they equal the homogenous teams. But a couple of studies suggested and a wealth of anecdotal evidence suggested a slightly different story. Diverse teams tend to perform either better or worse than homogenous ones, with more performing worse than better."*

In other words, diversity in global teams does not per se lead to high performance. Quite to the contrary, it can lead to diverse teams performing worse than homogenous ones. Intriguing, isn't it?

Based on this observation, the authors then studied multicultural teams with qualitative methods in order to identify critical factors for developing high performance. During their research they realized that **global teams come in three performance categories**. These team performance clusters are distinguished by the team's ability to deal with cultural differences and include:

- **The Destroyers:** Destroying teams perceive cultural differences as cultural traits leading to behaviours that are of less value compared to their own cultural strategies to solve problems, for example. Sometimes, destroyers perceive cultural diversity as a threat, which may even cause physical symptoms typical of anxiety (such as increased sweating or an accelerated heart rate) whenever they have to communicate with "them". Needless to say, performance fuelled by cultural anxiety is almost always poor since diversity can never be used as a valuable resource.

- **The Equalizers:** Equalizing teams ignore cultural differences and focus on similarities, pretending all runs smoothly. However, this attitude will often reflect a "friendly avoidance" of dealing with conflict and very often lead to disadvantageous compromises. Always seeking the smallest common denominator, these teams therefore tend to perform at mediocre levels.

- **The Creators:** In creator teams, *"differences are explicitly recognized and accepted, even nurtured, and their implications are incorporated into every facet of the group's processes. Watching these teams is like watching a top-performing jazz ensemble."*[9] Creators are what we need to achieve high performance in diverse virtual teams.

The following image contains a sketch of these results.

Figure 1.2: Diversity as a Team Challenge

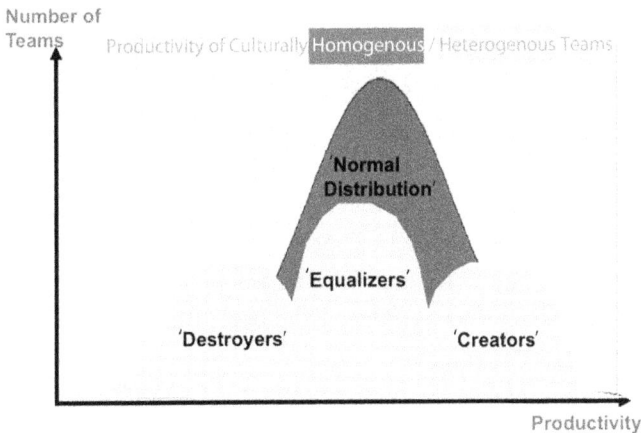

Adapted from Organizational Dynamics, 29(1), DiStefano, J. and Maznevski, M.L., Creating value with diverse teams in global management, p. 45–63, Copyright 2000, with permission from Elsevier.

Global groups are in need of high levels of tolerance and appreciation of diversity in order to perform as well or outperform collocated and/ or culturally homogeneous teams.

Success factor # 2: Using technology to simulate reality → *Getting closer in the virtual cloud*

The second success factor lies in getting closer "in the virtual cloud", meaning using available technology optimally to simulate or even enhance reality as much as possible.

The goal is to reduce the feeling of physical separation through working with Skype, SharePoint, or other platforms. Particularly the use of visual technology can create a situation very similar to one in which people are physically in the same location. Apart from video technology, this can be done with second life technology[10] using avatars (for advanced users) or including graphic online facilitation and the use of photos, widgets, or drawings. In Chapter Eight, we will discuss media and technology in more detail.

> ➢ One small but illustrating real-world example of such simulation is the water-cooler or coffee-machine experience: when working virtually in smaller groups and using web-(video)conferencing software, members can take their laptops with built-in webcams with them while getting water or coffee. This form of informal communication will give the far-flung colleagues an idea of the others' environment and a sense of their office routine. In fact, organizations have realized how important coffee machines and other communal areas are, both for collocated and virtual work. The psychological wisdom on the importance of informal office communications has informed the design of many contemporary workspaces.

Success factor # 3: Holding the team together → Getting closer as a group

Regular, coherent, intense and authentic communication is key when virtual groups are working to get closer. So is agreeing to a common language to ensure understanding one another. This success factor is highly dependent on the kind of virtual leadership mentioned earlier, which we will discuss in depth in Chapter Three. We feel close when we are comfortable with each other, when we are part of an authentic, honest whole that follows its own rhythm of interaction in a shared space. It is the leader's task to protect group members and to orchestrate group activities within a frame that makes members want to be part of the group. Beyond that, it is also the leader's responsibility to make it every member's task to share leadership and cultivate the shared space. The concept of Shared Leadership, which is crucial to the success of virtual groups, will be discussed in Chapter Two.

> ➢ In many cultures, from the Arabian Peninsula all the way to Los Angeles, it is a given for a good manager to know about the private conditions (i.e. family, birthdays, special events in the life of a person) of his or her group members. This knowledge is included in everyday work life, for example through an event calendar. Another great way to create Virtual Closeness in groups is to start meetings with the mutual sharing of private news and a bit of office gossip. This "insider" information helps group members to bond and feel connected.
>
> Both examples require the investment of precious time, which can be difficult for very busy groups. However, investing time into creating Virtual Closeness is rewarded by an increased identification of members with their group and the group's goals and objectives. Overall participation in meetings and increased commitment often follow.

Virtual Closeness and Trust

Another concept that is central to working with (virtual) groups is that of trust. Trust is a key element of building authentic relationships as a basis for successful virtual cooperation. Earlier we have defined

Virtual Closeness by means of delineating it from virtual distance as another way of improving virtual collaboration. Similarly, we will now look at Virtual Closeness as it relates to building trust and explain why and how Virtual Closeness operationalizes trust, thus making for a more practical and easier-to-use coaching tool.

Informed by a large body of management literature, managers are usually advised by consultants to focus on building trust in their teams. But the question remains how trust is actually fabricated. It is an emotional phenomenon, which depends on each individual's life experience with trusting the self and others. Trust cannot be ordered. Yes, we can send teams on adventures, such as team climbing, hoping that, once outside of their comfort zones, they will open up to one another. But whether or not people trust each other defies measurement or control. A leader can't expect his employees to trust each other but she/he can work with the operational and measurable dimensions of Virtual Closeness and, if all goes well, trust will form in consequence. Additionally, trust means a lot of different things in different cultures.

> *Example: Culture-specific Push and Pull*

According to our surveys, one of the key German work values always ranking among the top three is *Zuverlässigkeit*. English dictionaries tend to offer between three and five different definitions or translations of *Zuverlässigkeit*. A Spanish dictionary may contain up to eight. This indicates that the particular value of *Zuverlässigkeit* is a culturally unique conglomerate of various value factors, which are hard to transfer directly into other cultural contexts.

We know of similar phenomena in other cultures/languages, such as the Brazilian *jeitinho* * or the Chinese guanxi†. *The linguistic root of Zuverlässigkeit* means "you can leave me with it" – no need to check or follow up. When Germans want to prove that they are *zuverlässig*, they will not only deliver on time

---

* To spin or turn things to enable solutions that satisfy everyone involved. In practice, this means granting each other exceptions, which is similar to the Chinese concept of *guanxi* in certain aspects.

† The deliberate development of mutual dependencies through doing each other favours.

and with the agreed upon quality but also without reminders or other means of outside monitoring. Because they are expected to deliver, i.e. "push" their working tasks, asking them about their work progress several times within the agreed-upon time frame may imply a lack of trust.

In many Asian cultures, on the contrary, the process owner who delegates the task is expected to demand actively (i.e. "pull") the contributions from group members. The indications for trust are reversed. If the process owner does not follow up at regular intervals, it might be very hard for the person who has taken the responsibility for the task to develop a trustful relationship to the person who delegated the task. By continuously pulling the required contribution, those delegating help to avoid conflict.

The Relation of Virtual Closeness and Trust

Let us now look at how Virtual Closeness and trust relate, starting with the similarities.

Trust exists in two forms[11]:

- Personal trust between people and
- Organizational or abstract trust in institutional structures.

The same applies to Virtual Closeness. Both concepts – personalized and abstract identification – are probably *the* most important prerequisites for developing high performance in virtual collaboration settings. However, we argue that there is no causal relation between trust and high performance. People may trust each other, but that doesn't mean they will perform well because of that. Developing Virtual Closeness, on the other hand, includes forging trust to create a framework wherein high performance can grow.

Figure 1.3: Trust and Virtual Closeness

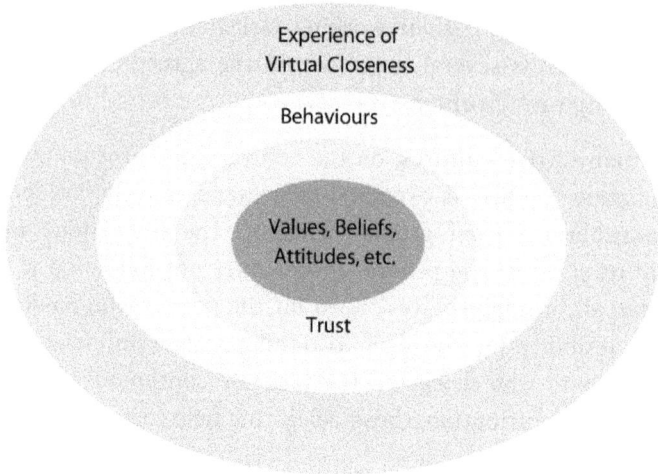

Causality does exist the other way around, though. If a virtually working group lacks Virtual Closeness or trust, they are unlikely to reach levels of high performance.

➤ Two people trust each other, but are not virtually close. Both assume that the other is competent to make a valuable contribution to the team. Using email as their main communication channel, however, creates frustration because, due to the lack of an open discussion about everyone's communication needs, neither one is addressing these. They lack Virtual Closeness.

On the other hand, consider the following example.

➤ A enjoys working with B. She appreciates B's ways of writing emails and likes having phone conversations with him. They feel virtually close. Due to specific circumstances in B's office, their communication is impeded. B's supervisor frequently interrupts B's calls with A, asking B to react to his demands immediately. The results of A and B's common work are delayed because B can't deliver on time due to the additional demands placed on him. His emails so appreciated by A no longer arrive in their usual quality, let alone at the promised time. Virtual Closeness between A and B is decreased and transformed into virtual distance.

These examples show that the concepts of trust and Virtual Closeness both include elements that are independent of each other. While there may be significant overlap, the presence of one doesn't guarantee that of the other. Therefore, Virtual Closeness and trust are *not* two sides of the same coin. Rather, trust is related to the attitudes, values and identity of a person and therefore difficult to influence and manage in a business context. Facing media and intercultural issues, the trust framework can quickly become too complex to handle in view of organizational priorities. Trust is an inherently messy and complex phenomenon. It is formed in highly individualized processes that largely depend on our unconscious blueprints. Artificially implementing or training as well as controlling trust within a team is very difficult and often impossible.

According to Nandhakumar and Baskerville[12], abstract trust in organizational processes and structures alone is not enough to make members of virtual teams feel comfortable and confident given its impersonalized nature. Personalized trust relationships are therefore sought to establish a feeling of true, human connection. However, building personal trust requires regular physical, face-to-face interaction with the other to get to know and be reassured by their body language and silent communication cues. For virtual teams, such physical interaction is usually rare and, if at all possible, comes at high costs. Therefore, relying on building trust to create high performing virtual teams seems to be ineffective.

In contrast, as discussed earlier, we believe that closeness, and thereby trust, can be built and experienced virtually without any physical interaction. Operating with Virtual Closeness, virtual groups are glued together while allowing their members to stay where they are.

> ➤ We always recommend to our clients that they create Virtual Closeness in the respective group *before* its first face-to-face meeting. This will ensure that precious face-to-face time is not used for basic relationship building but to get the work done. This increases efficiency and saves travel costs.

As visualized in the image above, Virtual Closeness thus operation-alizes and encompasses trust as a more practical management tool. Virtual Closeness is a state defined by a specific number of palpable, measurable indicators, which break down the factors of virtual team-work into small, directly trainable increments.

Nonetheless, in workshops of limited duration (two to four hours), or if the corporate values include trust, we sometimes do use the concept of trust to work on questions of virtual cooperation. While everyone has an inherent idea about trust, Virtual Closeness is a novel concept that requires some time to be introduced and understood.

When working with trust, we draw on the excellent concept of person-alized trust by WorldWork that is also based on the conviction that trust can be built virtually[13]. Unfortunately, the concept of abstract trust vis-à-vis organizations, processes, and structures – an element central to our approach to Virtual Closeness – is not contained in the WorldWork approach.

1.3 Virtual Performance Assessment (VPA) at a Glance

Making virtual collaboration work is a continuous process of improving group performance. The Virtual Performance Assessment (VPA) is designed to do exactly that. Informed by our experience of working with virtual teams, groups, and networks, our aim has been to develop a hands-on, pragmatic toolbox of great practical use to the daily reality of virtual groups.

VPA is a systemic approach to working with any unit of an organiza-tion and with the whole range of organizational stakeholders: senior managers, line managers, teams, groups, and networks. Holistic by design, VPA mirrors the systemic complexity of virtual groups. It integrates all organizational dimensions including relationships, the factual, and the organizational. In its comprehensiveness, VPA exceeds all other existing virtual performance improvement approaches, which mainly intervene on the group level, media or technology and tend to ignore vital aspects such as the organizational embedding.

The VPA framework consists of five categories wherein Virtual Closeness can be built and performance improved: Inclusion; Organization and Process; Space and Time; E-Culture; and Members, Tasks, and Objectives.

Introduction to VPA Categories and Dimensions

Textbox 1.3: VPA Categories

To map virtual performance and provide the basis for Purple Spaces, we have developed a comprehensive assessment tool, the Virtual Performance Assessment (VPA). VPA maps virtual performance in twenty dimensions grouped into five categories.

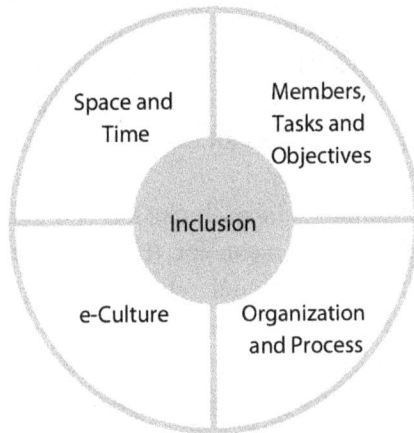

In all five categories, we have identified concrete success criteria for communication and collaboration in an intercultural and virtual working context. Those success criteria translate into four dimensions per category – a total of twenty dimensions. The categories and the corresponding dimensions were tested numerous times in direct collaboration with virtual groups. After evaluating their feedback, some dimensions were collapsed and others were added or rephrased, until we ended up with the current model.

In the following section, we will introduce the five categories and twenty dimensions of VPA. All five categories and twenty dimensions are discussed in detail in chapters two to six.

VPA is a modular system of categories that provide a framework wherein Virtual Closeness and the corresponding Purple Space, as prerequisites for high performance, are built and maintained. Each category is the product of the interplay of the respective four sub-dimensions. In other words, each of the five categories is broken down into four dimensions, which combine, overlap and intersect to map and define the category. In this grid system lies the pragmatic quality of VPA and, thus, of Virtual Closeness.

The five categories are differentiated to the extent that they can be used as discrete modular interventions, given that each category covers a different topic area. To make VPA as practical as possible, we have designed and distinguished the categories in a way that allows locating hot spots of improvement needs and starting in-depth "helicopter" interventions exactly there. VPA therefore allows screening group situations in a more reflected, structured, and operational way. Obviously, one can also work in all categories simultaneously.

As presented in the image above, Inclusion is a compulsory element of each VPA process. The reason for this focus is that Inclusion is intimately linked to interpersonal relationships and cultural diversity, and thus key to unlocking the potential lying therein. The four dimensions in the Inclusion category are *Shared Leadership, Feedback Competence, Communication Styles*, and *Work Styles*. They lie at the very heart of creating Virtual Closeness and the corresponding Purple Space. In the organizational context they fall in the realm of relationships and attitude – a realm of obvious significance to feeling virtually close. The other four categories can be included in a VPA process depending on the respective organizational and technical context and time constrictions.

Notes

1   Ferrazzi (2012); Siebdrat et al. (2009); Majchrzak et al. (2004).
2   Majchrzak et al. (2004).
3   Forchhammer (2012).
4   See Note 2, above.
5   Lojeski and Reilly (2008).
6   Ibid.

7   Majchrzak et al. (2004).
8   DiStefano and Maznevski (2000).
9   Ibid.
10 Second Life Technology creates three-dimensional virtual worlds "populated" (i.e. brought to life) by avatars. It is a very useful tool for the visual simulation of reality in virtual collaboration.
11 Nandhakumar and Baskerville (2001).
12 Ibid.
13 http://www.worldwork.biz/legacy/www/docs3/itti3.html.

• •

The Story Begins

In order to help you apply the content of this book, we have written a case study in story format based on our experiences of working with global virtual teams, groups, and networks. This case study frames chapters two to six, each of which is devoted to one of the categories of Virtual Closeness.

The case study is designed to give you a practical understanding of the different categories and dimensions of Virtual Closeness and the corresponding Purple Space. It is also intended to encourage targeted reflection at the end of every chapter through asking questions in the following two categories:

- Have I gained a practical understanding of the different dimensions of Virtual Closeness?

- What would I do to support the fictitious group in improving their virtual performance? What are the levers? What could be suitable interventions?

The Storm Has Tripled

It seems that the storm has doubled, even tripled, in size. Florian Bell is standing in a Duty Free Shop in Dubai International Airport. Outside the tinted windows and against the low background hum of the air conditioning, the sand storm that will delay his departure indefinitely is rising. The sales rep regrets that the computer game, which Bell promised to bring back to Munich for his 16-year-old son, Kai, is not available in the Emirates.

An alternative to the usual ego shooters, the point of the game is to disentangle complex strands of action in sand-storm-ridden Dubai. At least this is what Kai told him, and his younger brother, Max, had eagerly nodded in agreement. The boys thought it was cool that their father was now regularly travelling to the desert.

"The authorities have forbidden it here", the customer standing next to him whispers with a strong Indian accent. "Criticism disturbs them in selling their dream". "Oh really", Bell responds. He isn't in the mood for a discussion about Dubai's economic or moral state. The storm re-enters his awareness on his way to the lounge as he passes the large airport windows. It reminds him of a vacuum which sucks in everything that doesn't belong here.

In his head, a different kind of storm is rising, the third of the day. Six months earlier, when his manager, Ulf Moser, told him about the company's plan to move the Interior Electronics department to the Gulf, he was shocked at first. Beltronik (Bavarian Electronics, formerly BE, Bavarian Electrics) used to be proud of its 103-year-old tradition. Founded in a suburb of Munich, the company had developed into a global brand with 28,000 employees in 35 locations spread over 13 countries and an annual turnover of 3.1 billion Euro.

A producer of high-quality electronic components, Beltronik offers products and solutions along the whole value chain. The broad client base includes the automotive, facility management, and medical technology industries as well as individual consumers. Faced with massive low-priced competition from Asia, the company was hit by a sales crisis at the beginning of the new millennium. Rescue came from the Emirati federal investment fund "Al Noor" ("The Light") based in Dubai, which currently holds one-third of Beltronik's corporate shares.

The official narrative underlying the Arabic investment is based on diversifying the local economy and developing knowledge hubs in preparation for the post-oil era. In Munich, however, rumor has it that Interior Electronics doesn't really fit in the fund's portfolio and that improved results are urgently needed in the short run to avoid upsetting the investor.

During the past two years, Beltronik has been implementing a comprehensive change process, including a global matrix structure, in order to adapt to international complexities and create leaner processes. In a next step, the board decided to internationalize the company altogether and, for a start, moved part of the leadership team of the Interior Electronics department that delivers supply to clients in the automotive and medical technology industries to Dubai. As a member of the leadership team, Bell will coordinate the setup processes on-site in Dubai during the first two months and travel to the Gulf frequently thereafter.

Management has officially explained this move as being due to the benefit of being closer to Asian clients, markets, and power hubs and, at the same time, has wanted to signal to the investors how much Munich values the partnership. However, Bell's supervisor, Ulf Moser, has confided to him that it is in fact a test run for moving further business units to the Gulf in the medium term, with the possibility of only keeping parts of the administration and research and development departments in Munich.

Bell sinks into the white plush of the lounge chair. On the screen above him, pixels continuously reassemble into changing patterns. During the two months ahead, he will be challenged with new and similarly complex constellations. In addition to building and leading a small team in Dubai, his task is to keep the local stakeholders on Beltronik's side. Besides, he will have to cope with the demands of his family. His wife, Ina, isn't happy about the fact that Bell will be working from Dubai for the next couple of months and regularly travelling to the city thereafter. Family life has been a high priority for the Bells but, with Florian's new role, this will be difficult to maintain.

During his absence, he'll continue supervising the 15 colleagues who report to him at headquarters in Munich and who function as focal points for 40 local retail managers in the different regions. This will be interesting. While he has been macro managing his team so far, he imagines that the distance will require him to tighten supervision, especially as he will be travelling to the Gulf at least once a month after the initial two-month on-site period. At the same time, he already worries that his colleagues in Dubai might not feel sufficiently led and could soon demand his increased presence beyond a few days a month.

His manager, Moser, will remain in Munich, too; and probably, this will be one of the main challenges once Bell is frequently away on mission. He considers himself to be fairly young for the job and knows that he'll have to make sure to stay close enough to the power centres around the second- and third-tier leaders. He also knows that management is observing what some call "The Gulf Experiment" rather suspiciously.

Against this backdrop, the demands of the "Global Virtual Quality Circle" seem like a piece of cake. Founded by the board, the purpose of this circle is to develop strategies to advance corporate virtual communications within the next 12 months. So far, IT departments in the various countries and regions have provided different standards of communication and collaboration technology, with different levels of maturity, and infrastructure to the teams, let alone informal local practices. The circle was deployed to harmonize those practices and placed under Bell's responsibility to emphasize the central role Dubai will play from now on.

Outside the lounge windows, the storm disappears as rapidly as it rose. Within minutes, the colour of the sky turns into an almost supernatural blue, interspersed with light yellow streaks. Bell searches the screen for information about his flight. "If only things came together as easily over the coming months as they did just now", he thinks, as he spots his flight and starts walking.

●●●

Inclusion

2.1   The Four Dimensions of Inclusion

2.2   The Story: The First Encounter

2.3   Feedback Competence

2.4   Communication Styles

2.5   Work Styles

2.6   Shared Leadership

2.7   Self Reflection: Lessons Learned from Chapter Two

2.8   Coaching Questions for Inclusion

2.1 The Four Dimensions of Inclusion

This category examines the vital dimensions which ensure that members feel included in a group, thus unlocking the potential of diversity.

Communication
Styles

Shared
Leadership   **Inclusion**   Work
Styles

Feedback
Competence

In our experience, inclusion of human diversity is the central issue in nearly every virtual group. When virtual groups are formed, often (very) different kinds of *Communication Styles* and *Work Styles* come together in the shared interaction space. According to the different modes of intercultural competence in groups – recall the Destroyers, Equalizers, and Creators of Chapter One – coping with such diversity basically follows one of two options: integration (if someone feels excluded from the group) or inclusion (where every group member feels like a valuable part of the group from the beginning); with the inability to cope with diversity as a third "option". Creating an enabling environment for inclusion and the feeling of belonging to a Purple Space is a leadership task that must not be bound to one particular person but rather rest on *Shared Leadership* and the *Feedback Competence* of each group member, including, of course, the team leader.

In most virtual groups operating internationally, 1+1 is less than 2 (< 2). In the cultural context, integration means that the different, the foreign is adapted to the main culture so that the latter largely remains the same. The foreign continues to exist, often in parallel, but it adds little or no new value to the main culture.

The equation for inclusion, on the contrary, says that 1+1 is more than two (> 2). The result is more than the added factors. How is this possible? Clearly, high performance happens in the Creator groups because they are able to, well: create. Creating is the making of something new that is more than what exists, thereby adding value. Two different approaches are mined for their values and an emerging third way is negotiated, thereby reducing the overall complexity. The added value is greater than the sum of the single parts. Reduced complexity is a characteristic feature of trans-cultural approaches and defines our concept of Purple Space.

This is how diversity is best coped with: by using differences, as scary and overwhelming as they might at first appear, to create a culture and a shared interaction space wherein that culture is embedded that give them a right to exist and combine their best aspects. Rather than copying and pasting a preferred set of cultural norms, inclusion happens at the interface of the differences between people and their approaches to work. Inclusion requires a manager's and/or leader's ability to negotiate norms that are shared by the different group members.

These shared norms make up the social aspects of the Purple Space. Inclusion means that the local (the "blue" and "red") spaces of working continue to exist and are complemented by an additional, new space of belonging: the "purple" space. Shared norms for the Purple Space are created through negotiation and through leadership decisions. Members of virtual groups work in both spaces – in their local world when operating on the home front and in the purple when collaborating and communicating in the global part of their work. They move in and out of both worlds as the respective project work demands it.

> When two (or more) very different companies fuse or when one is taken over by a host with a different culture, it is precisely the fusion of the differences and the resulting newness that adds value to what was there before. However, when a new culture is not actively developed from the get-go, this potential is often lost in the process. In fact, the organizational life of a company that has been taken over, for example, can quickly develop "antibodies" to the

host culture when organizational cultural development is lacking. Not feeling seen and appreciated, employees then either go into friendly avoidance mode or into resignation.

➢ The above can turn into a veritable paradox when one company decides to buy another because the purchased company has something the buyer is lacking. In many the case of many takeovers, the purchasing company's culture patronizes and eventually erases the other culture. This is contrary to the initial goal of acquiring the other, which happened precisely because of wanting what the other had. So the task is to preserve the cultural idiosyncrasies of the new member in the organizational system while creating an inclusive, new culture.

The goal of creating inclusion is that everyone feels included in the group and the virtual collaboration space *with* all their personal characteristics, not excluded because of them. People are part of the whole group while keeping their defining specific characteristics. This creates a feeling of belonging which, in turn, empowers group members to act and make decisions that benefit the whole group.

Meeting face-to-face often makes working together easier. When getting to know the other group members, people often feel that they belong to the group. And this leads to a crucial aspect: people usually take on a higher level of commitment. Once a person bonds personally with her colleagues, she is likely to respond to their emails. Ignoring them is no longer an option.

The task for virtual groups is to create that level of commitment in virtuality. Virtual Closeness paves the road for this. We will show in Chapter Eight that this forming can indeed be done using the right media without meeting face-to-face.

2.2 The Story: The First Encounter

Snow is falling from a slate grey sky. From his window, Bell gazes at the suburb of Munich, where Beltronik moved its headquarters a decade ago after the old office had become too small. His eyes rest on an industrial park that could be located anywhere in the world.

The phone conference to kick off the "Virtual Quality Circle" is scheduled to start in less than ten minutes. Initially he had planned to use the new video-conferencing technology that has been installed in every meeting room of the Munich headquarters, but not in all of the other global locations.

Next to a glass of water, Bell has put his notes about the members of the circle to help him structure the meeting and "meet the participants where they are". This seems particularly important given that the choice of "team" members has not only been explicitly cross-cultural but also cross-functional in order to ensure representation of multiple perspectives:

- Ranjit Gupta (Chennai)
  46, married, 3 children, 9 years with Beltronik, Director IT India

- Britt Svensson (Gothenburg)
  39, lives in civil union, 2 school-aged children from a previous marriage, 6 years with Beltronik, Global Marketing Manager

- Huy Yuan (Beijing)
  32, unmarried, 1 year with Beltronik, Logistics Manager China

- Kenji Sakamoto (Tokyo)
  56, married, 1 child, 18 years with Beltronik, Vice President Operations Japan

- Paolo Azevedo (Sao Paulo)
  36, married, 2 children, 3 months with Beltronik, Sales Manager Latin America

- Patricia Kennedy (Atlanta)
  Age? 0 entries in database, no family status, moved from HQ to Atlanta with management approval, sick mother, 16 years with Beltronik, Vice President Global HR

Bell sent out a slide with the meeting agenda to all participants prior to the meeting:

- 12:00 Welcome
- 12:05 Introduction round
- 12:15 First sharing of local practice
- 12:45 Agree on project steps and time frame
- 12:55 Action items
- 13:00 Sign out

Before the meeting starts, Bell receives an SMS from Gupta who congratulates him on being appointed leader of the Quality Circle: "Please accept my heartfelt congratulations. Can we speak after the meeting? Rgds Ranjit".

Bell decides to reply later because he wants to concentrate on the meeting for now.

One after another the participants dial in and are greeted by Bell. At noon, all members except for Huy Yuan are there.

Bell: "Welcome everybody to our first Global Virtual Quality Circle meeting. Some of you already know me in person, but most of you only through emails or from the phone. I look forward to having the chance to meet all of you personally as soon as possible."

Svensson (chuckles): "Hey Florian, we need you to be more positive and motivational about our virtuality, especially since we should practice what we preach…"

Bell: "Well, yes, you're right, Britt, I'll give my best. On another note, Huy Yuan is still missing. I'll briefly send him a message to check where he is."

Svensson: "Shall we continue in the meantime?"

Bell: "Uhm, go ahead…"

Svensson: "I'm Britt Svensson, Global Marketing Manager located in Gothenburg and the world, as my four children would say when I pick them up from their schools and continue to be on my cell for Beltronik's global marketing efforts in spite of being already off work – officially."

Bell: "Thank you for taking over, Britt. Huy has just sent me a message that he'll try to be with us a little later on."

Bell isn't overly satisfied with how the phone conference goes. Members introduce themselves in very different ways, which Bell credits to the cultural variety, among other reasons. Paolo Azevedo, for example, who only recently joined the company, takes his sweet time to introduce himself enthusiastically and very personally, while Kenji Sakamoto says no more than three sentences about himself, despite his seniority.

A first discussion about local practices regarding media usage and virtual communication shows the differences across the company. Patricia Kennedy and Britt Svensson take the lead in this part of the meeting.

Kennedy reports on the measures taken to counter email flooding: "You know, some of us receive what – a hundred, a hundred-and-fifty mails a day – and our CIO decided that we should follow the example of some American companies and prohibit internal 'thank you' mails."

Svensson: "Wow, that is incredible, now you can't even say 'thank you' any more to your colleagues…"

Kennedy: "Yeah, but about only half of the staff really followed that policy."

Meanwhile, Gupta sends him another SMS: "Did you try to get hold of Yuan's boss?", and: "May I advise you to bring in Sakamoto more?"

When Azevedo shares the local practice in the Sao Paulo office, which clearly centres on phone and chat, Gupta responds enthusiastically: "We love chat in India, since we are such chatty people."

Counters Svensson: "I personally would appreciate it if you would not interrupt the reports, Ranjit. We only have half an hour left in our call."

Bell is trying to consolidate the various contributions and, wanting to involve Sakamoto in the conversation, asks him whether he also uses chat. After a longer pause, Sakamoto answers: "I prefer other ways of communicating."

Kennedy asks: "Who, by the way, takes the minutes?"

Immediately, Bell answers: "I've been keeping notes."

Kennedy: "Great, Florian, but you don't need to do everything. Let us know if you want somebody to take over."

Bell: "Thank you Patricia, that is very kind of you. Ah, I see that Huy Yuan is also with us! Welcome Huy, can you hear us well? Huy?"

Yuan: "Yes, Mister Bell?"

Bell: "Huy, we have missed you and hope everything is okay on your side?"

Yuan: "Yes, all okay."

Bell: "We've been sharing local practice. What can you tell us about yours in China?"

Yuan: "I will speak with my colleagues and next time I give the report."

Kennedy: "But we are certain that you can share a bit of what you yourself use on a day-to-day basis."

Gupta: "We can also wait, there is no need to rush. I would rather have Huy ask around a bit more and have him report next time."

Simultaneously, Bell receives yet another SMS from Gupta: "Need to take Yuan off stage."

At the end of the conference, there is just enough time to decide when the next meeting will take place and to distribute action items. While participants say their goodbyes, Bell's manager, Ulf Moser, is already waiting at the door. As usual, he appears without warning.

Moser: "You just had the first Circle meeting, didn't you? How did it go?"

Bell: "Okay, though a bit chaotic. But I guess that's to be expected when seven grownups from different countries, who hardly or don't know each other, attempt to achieve results during a phone conference. I need to better organize the next meeting."

Moser: "I'm sure you'll manage, Bell. Let me know how I can support you. We really need to work on the board presentation now. Our meeting about that with Hallhuber starts in a few minutes. Are you coming?"

Outside, the sky has cleared a little and the snowfall lessened, appearing to descend in slow motion now. Bell and Moser stepped into the hall. Didn't Gupta ask Bell in his first text message to speak to him right after the phone conference?

Throughout chapters Two to Six, the sections that will introduce the different dimensions of Virtual Closeness follow a particular structure. In a textbox, we share the respective definition and present and explain the two defining items of each dimension that we also use to help users of our VPA tool to understand the assessment questions. This is followed by examples of good practice and some advice on how to create Virtual Closeness in the respective dimension.

2.3 Feedback Competence

When working with groups, we usually start by looking at this dimension: the level of voicing and Feedback Competence in a group. Addressing a group's "hot topics" without having a shared culture of voicing important issues in place is very difficult. A voicing culture is also the basis for negotiating the norms of interacting in the Purple Space. Feedback, on the other hand, builds on this ability and willingness to voice. However, feedback usually focuses on the behaviour of others and is intended to initiate a behavioural change as desired by the feedback giver. In being a more open process and touching also abstract issues, voicing is therefore more general than feedback. That said, we'll use the concepts of voicing and feedback interchangeably as together they form a specific group culture.

> ### Textbox 2.1: Definition: Dimension "Feedback Competence"
>
> The degree to which a supportive feedback culture is established.
>
> *Item 1: The degree to which members are open to exchange work-related, informal feedback.*
>
> This item addresses questions like: Do members proactively give and seek feedback? Do all members take part in providing and seeking feedback? Is feedback also provided proactively to management and other members? Does the group feel that they have a common understanding of how to give and receive feedback?
>
> *Item 2: The degree to which members proactively support a culture in which work-related, informal feedback is exchanged.*
>
> This item addresses questions like: Do members perceive feedback as something positive that can improve the group's performance? Do members take the possibly diverse feedback practices of members into account? Are people from different cultural backgrounds aware of the potential growth that feedback can offer?

Good Practice

Many leaders still believe that the absence of conflict and criticism in their groups is a good sign. In reality, the opposite is true. The absence of conflict often points to a state of friendly avoidance of other people or situations. In a virtual context, politely ignoring one another is much easier than in collocated settings.

Moreover, feedback styles and competences are determined by culture. In some cultures, any direct criticism is understood as an attack on a person's dignity while, in others, only direct comments and criticism are considered as feedback.

In order to get the most out of the complexity and cultural diversity of a global group, a high level of voicing and Feedback Competence on the part of all members is essential. Feedback as a crucial leadership competence is necessary in order to raise critical and positive aspects of cooperation as well as awareness of work and Communication Styles and shared responsibility among all group members.

In virtual settings, people can choose to avoid the other entirely. In the absence of talking to each other, problems can quickly grow out of proportion and lead to inertia. A state of fake tolerance is created. Consider the following model of the nine levels of not voicing an issue developed by Myrna Lewis[1]. They show what happens when a group member no longer feels comfortable because of a problem festering below the radar of communication.

Figure 2.1: The Nine Levels of Not Voicing

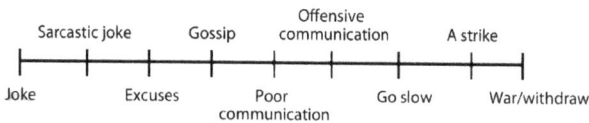

```
                                    Offensive
        Sarcastic joke    Gossip    communication      A strike
      ├──────┼──────┼──────┼──────┼──────┼──────┼──────┤
      Joke          Excuses       Poor         Go slow    War/withdraw
                              communication
```

Groups often enter this spiral without being conscious of what is happening and end up in a deadlock. Members lose motivation and the energy level necessary for good collaboration and disengage. Such dead ends can be avoided relatively easily when a culture of voicing is established early on in a group.

Remember Joseph DiStefano's and Martha Maznevski's performance categories from Chapter One:

Figure 2.2: Diversity as a Team Challenge

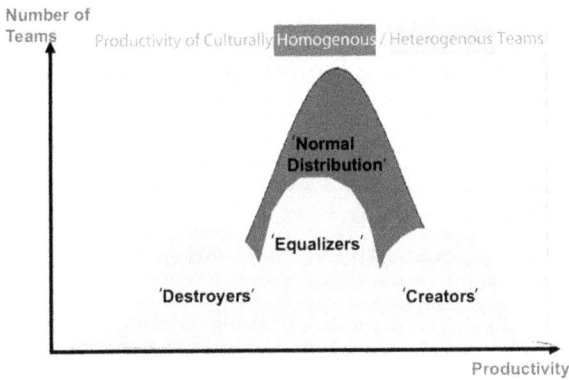

Adapted from Organizational Dynamics, 29(1), DiStefano, J. and Maznevski, M.L., Creating value with diverse teams in global management, p. 45–63, Copyright 2000, with permission from Elsevier.

The "Creator" teams are those that are explicitly aware of their diversity and actively build on it by establishing an effective habit of voicing and giving regular feedback.

Our Advice

The following checklist is useful when creating a voicing culture – a culture of flowing feedback.

✓ Feedback is understood as a regular and respectful way of voicing one's observations about all aspects of group work. It does not automatically mean negative criticism.

✓ Experiences, preferences, and expectations of feedback in a group are discussed. Is feedback considered a useful mechanism that helps the group excel and get closer? Or, based on negative past experiences, is feedback feared?

✓ Methods for giving and receiving feedback with which all members can identify are negotiated, including an understanding of individual boundaries – for example, when is feedback appreciated and when is it not well received? Available media are used as appropriate, depending on personal preferences. Feedback can be given via video or phone conference in the presence of all members as well as privately via email or chat.

✓ Feedback based on observation is given in three modes:
  • *Continue* – more of this!

  • *Start* – you are doing fine but please do more of x, y, or z.

  • *Stop* – no more!

✓ A culture of voicing and feedback is established and developed so that each member feels that he/she can give feedback to all colleagues, including the leaders, without fearing retribution.

➤ An international enterprise sets up a new virtual group for a high-priority R&D project. Members are located in five different countries. Once they start working together, they begin to realize the array of different work and Communication Styles in their group. These differences get in the way of working and communicating effectively, but the group has problems talking about this. How to intervene?

A shared responsibility for *wanting* to fix the situation needs to be created, or else the problem will remain unspoken. First, the group needs to develop a healthy habit of voicing and giving feedback to expose the problem. Voicing (responding in virtuality) is one of the first training sessions to which experienced global corporations subject their employees. In addition to defining and training voicing, it actually needs to be applied in daily work. Second, the specific way an issue is raised depends on the existing Feedback Competence. WHAT is voiced? Things that are linked to communication and Work Styles, not petty aspects like someone's looks. What ensues is a continual process of negotiation and communication among the group, facilitated by group members and the leader in a shared fashion (Shared Leadership).

2.4 Communication Styles

Often, once a group establishes a culture that allows its members to address anything of great importance to them, they realize that their different Communication Styles have a significant impact on how close members feel to each other.

The degree to which members are aware of different Communication Styles and proactively employ these in their communication.

Item 1: The degree to which members are aware of how their (culturally influenced) Communication Styles are perceived by others.

This item addresses questions like: Are members aware of their own Communication Styles? Do members know how other members perceive their way of communicating? Do members know how their way of communicating differs from that of other members? Do members know various ways of communicating that are linked to diverse cultural backgrounds in the group?

Item 2: The degree to which members are able to adjust their (culturally influenced) Communication Styles so that their messages are better understood by others.

This item addresses questions like: How flexible and customer-oriented are members when communicating across cultural boundaries? Are members able to adjust their ways of communicating, so their message is better understood by the reader or listener?

Good Practice

Few factors are as vital for Virtual Closeness as communication. Communication enables the necessary, smooth overlap of tasks to permit the interlocking of work processes which, in turn, creates a workflow. A virtual group is usually characterized by a variety of different Communication Styles. Such diversity is often challenging. The main question here is how to cope with that in a practical context.

In order to understand the diversity of cultural preferences in a group better, it is helpful to understand how dialogue patterns differ. When one participant in a dialogue is speaking, the other can either interrupt her or wait until she is finished with her statement, then either immediately start speaking or pause before speaking.

These three patterns are visualized in the following box.

Textbox 2.3: Example: Communication and Pause Patterns

The pattern of dialogues can differ significantly across cultural backgrounds, particularly regarding the pauses made between thoughts or different speakers.

The following three examples of dialogues between persons A and B show different cultural preferences for communication patterns. In an intercultural group, it is essential to understand these cultural differences in order to avoid or overcome frustration and misunderstanding about being interrupted or confronted with silences.

1 – Stop = Start cultures

A   ___   ___   ___

B   ___   ___

Members of cultures that consider time as a primary resource, including Germans or Swiss, tend to dislike pauses and find it difficult to bear them. They usually start speaking the moment the other person stops.

2 – Stop = Pause cultures

       __   __

A   ___   ___

         __   __

B   ___   ___

Members of cultures in which information is collected before taking the initiative and avoiding conflicts is imperative, such as in most Asian and some of the Nordic countries, tend to pause between thoughts or speakers. They do this to show that they reflect on what's been said and to allow the other to finish his/her thought. Accepting that pause and being able to bear short periods of silence can be challenging for colleagues from the other cultures.

3 – Taking over = Stop cultures

A   ___   ___   ___   ___

B   ___   ___   ___

In cultures that value relationships as a primary resource, such as Spain or Brazil, talking over one another is common. Often, people don't wait for a speaker to finish his or her thought. Interruptions are part of the conversational nature. They signal that the one interrupting understood what was said and is now ready to respond. Such a dynamic dialogue is a sign of a good relationship.

Now imagine a phone conference with members of dialogue cultures 2 and 3, such as a group of Brazilian and Chinese group members. After the conference you might hear the following complaints:

- The Chinese might complain that they had no chance to contribute because the Brazilians kept talking and interrupting each other. "Why did they invite us to the conference at all? They were not interested in our perspective on the issue."

- The Brazilians might complain that the Chinese didn't contribute to the conversation. "There is no point in inviting the Chinese colleagues because they never come up with ideas for problem solving. They always just listen."

This (typical) situation likely creates or perpetuates virtual distance and, thus, lowers performance. So, what to do?

Our Advice

Effective communication in global groups requires that they build a Purple Space of shared norms for how to communicate. Communication lies at the heart of creating Virtual Closeness and, in building a shared identity specifically for the purpose of virtual cooperation and communication, we fill the Purple Spaces with a common understanding of our differences. The concept of Purple Space is unique in that it transcends the raising of awareness, which tends to be standard in intercultural communication. It goes beyond that by creating a concrete practice of including the differences in a group.

The Team Clock

In diverse groups, phone conferences can be structured with the help of the right tools. Used in agendas, the team clock defines a sequence of speakers that is to be followed throughout the meeting. In a meeting, it reminds participants to address people personally and sequentially, one after the other.

In the example of the phone conference between the Brazilian and Chinese colleagues, the team clock is a tool that could be used to facilitate the coexistence of the different communication patterns explained above.

Figure 2.3: The Team Clock

In a call with more than five participants, using a team clock helps to structure members' airtime. Due to the clockwise rotation, they know exactly when they will be asked to speak. We recommend using the team clock three to five times during a session.

Direct or Indirect Language? Past-, Present-, or Future-oriented Argumentation Styles?

Communication Styles differ across cultures with respect to the context that is needed in order to decode a message. In cultures where communication is direct, the content of a message is usually exactly what is said. In cultures with an indirect Communication Style, the message can be more difficult to decode. Interpreting it will involve consideration of how and where it was uttered, what was omitted, which (and how) facial expressions and body gestures complemented the statement, and so forth.

People from the latter type of cultures often consider people from the former impolite or even rude. On the other hand, indirect communicators can be perceived by the others as vague, imprecise, and non-committal.

People also differ from each other in the ways they convince others. While some base their arguments on explaining past developments before considering their impact on present and future, others tend to stress the desired future outcome before explaining what has to be done in the present to achieve it. Still others focus on what needs doing now to manage challenges rooted in the past in order to achieve certain future outcomes.

Can you match these preferences with different cultures? Plough through your emails from German, US American, and Scandinavian colleagues for hints.

Coping with Different Communication Styles

When inviting members of a diverse group to a meeting, it is often unclear whether one ought to address the individual Communication Styles in a separate email to each invitee or send one email to the whole group. While the first option would be ideal, it is hardly doable in reality.

One solution for this dilemma is to write a future-oriented, indirect, polite invitation email that clearly outlines the framework of the meeting. The invitation should include a social dimension, for example a link to the meeting location or pictures from the last group meeting. Also, more detailed information about the meeting purpose and any necessary preparation should be included in direct language. This can be done with references to the context of a recent past such as an analysis of a situation that could be attached to the invitation in a separate document. For those members who need more social context and have greater informational needs, it is helpful to announce that there will be a time slot for talking about the context of the meeting.

To raise awareness about how different Communication Styles are perceived by others and how messages are transported in these different styles, we recommend working with an intercultural consultant.

2.5 Work Styles

Having established a shared voicing and feedback culture as well as efficient communication processes, the next step towards high performance is grappling with different Work Styles. We will look at the diversity of Work Styles in a group and how they can be leveraged to create innovative ways of collaborating.

Textbox 2.4: Definition: Dimension "Work Styles"

The degree to which members share an understanding of their work styles and are able to make them compatible if needed.

Item 1: The degree to which members are aware of how their (culturally influenced) work styles are perceived by others.

This item addresses questions like: Are members aware of their own work styles and the influence culture might have on them? Do members know how other members perceive their way of working? Do members know how their way of working differs from that of other members? Do members know various ways of working that are linked to diverse cultural backgrounds in the group?

Item 2: The degree to which members are able to adjust their (culturally influenced) work styles if needed in order to improve performance.

This item addresses questions like: How flexibly do members adapt their work style to the work style of other members? How well is the group able to take advantage of the potential offered by the different working styles? Does the group use the different working styles to improve its output?

Good Practice

Beliefs about how to work and what constitutes a "good" way of working, for example, may suddenly be challenged by different approaches in a dispersed intercultural group or even by customers from a new market. "How long do you plan and test before you rollout?" Instead of capitalizing on this diversity, many virtual groups are led locally. Managers tend to lead every group member individually according to their respective location instead of negotiating a leadership culture that suits all. This can be frustrating and ineffective.

One of the recurring issues is the belief that the local way of working is better than a global, centralized approach. Typical (explicit and implicit) relevant statements include:

- Our country figures speak for themselves

- Our culture has existed for more than a thousand years

- The people in our country are more satisfied with their life.

Clearly, measuring cultural elements with indicators that are part of the value system of one culture is a biased approach and is likely to lead to increasingly negative attitudes about other Work Styles.

Good practice should therefore be aimed at creating awareness that every work style can be successful, efficient, and effective in the context where it has been developed historically. If transferred to different cultural contexts, however, it can provoke disastrous conflict.

Once a group has developed a positive attitude towards diversity in Work Styles it can begin to create a shared collaboration space wherein different Work Styles are intentionally applied to relevant contexts as needed. In some markets, for example, it is advisable to move into the rollout phase as quickly as possible and adjust the product in an intensive communication process jointly with the customer, as opposed to introducing a high quality but standard product later.

Our Advice

When working with groups, it is important to start with those group processes that are most likely to unlock the greatest potential for saving time and creating commitment. The following are two examples from our work.

> **Decision Making**
> The term "decision" has different meanings across cultures. In some, a decision is understood to be final and no longer open to questioning. It is an agreement that demands immediate implementation. In others, it is a step on the way towards a final decision

and forms the basis for further discussion. In other environments, a decision will be considered only if the implementation has been discussed and agreed on with the majority of stakeholders beforehand. Global groups need to define a common understanding of what "decision" shall mean in their context in order to avoid confusion and frustration. If they try to integrate all involved cultures, they will quickly reach a point of unproductiveness. Agreeing upon a mutual meaning of decision is an example of a shared norm that defines the Purple Space of collaboration and reduces the complexity of possible definitions to one or only a few. It is a non-negotiable standard for the individual global group that exists along with all local practices.

> **Meeting Culture**
> Meeting cultures, too, differ significantly across countries. While in some cultures a meeting is an event dedicated to decision making and problem solving, in others it is used to communicate and celebrate decisions already made. Differences also exist between formal and informal meeting settings. Creating purple meeting spaces that are shared by colleagues across the globe is a major step towards global business efficiency. We have begun to work on that with a number of international companies. In contemporary business, people spend a lot of time in meetings and often feel that it is time wasted. Shaping an organization's meeting culture to unlock the participative potential of members has a great impact on the organization's overall culture, on cost saving, and on employee motivation.

As discussed earlier, raising awareness about the existing diversity in a group is an essential first step when seeking to create a shared culture. It is helpful to create an environment wherein the different Work Styles of a group can be present. This allows members of different cultures to put themselves in the shoes of those with different cultural preferences.

The following exercise intends to forge a positive attitude towards different Work Styles. Note that it works best when there are not more than three or four cultures present in a group.

✓ Group members are sent into three or four corners, or virtual spaces, that represent the three or four Work Styles present in the room and that are different from their own cultural background. They are asked to imagine the work style of the respective culture and to put themselves in the situation of people from that culture to help them understand what they need to experience in order to contribute to building a shared culture. That way, Swedish group members might be in the German corner, or virtual space, and gain a better understanding of their German colleagues' needs. Vice versa, German group members are sent into the Swedish space and get their Swedish co-workers' perspective.

The following textbox contains some typical examples of questions that we encounter frequently in the above exercise. The questions represent typical challenges for members from the respective culture. The questions are answered with exemplary conditions that would support an improved collaboration in diverse groups.

Textbox 2.5: Work Styles: Typical Questions and Possible Answers

Typical questions that arise when creating a shared approach to Work Styles and possible answers from different cultures

✓ How can you become more reliable and deliver on time? – When I start drawing on my network and making effective use of the resources and support it offers, I am able to manage my project much better. I don't need to do everything alone and am empowered to focus my energies selectively.

✓ What do you need in order to take the initiative? – We need guidance and clarity. What is expected of us? What are the quality indicators against which our contributions are measured?

✓ How can top workers be motivated to plan less and be more flexible? – If we define "product prototype" and "rollout" differently, we can gain more flexibility in our thinking about those concepts. The prototype differs from the product in that it can be imperfect. A rollout is done for the product, not for the prototype. This gives dealing with the prototype even more flexibility.

2.6 Shared Leadership

For a leader of a global virtual group it is practically impossible always to know what is going on in the different locations. When he wants to discuss a member's low performance, for example, it is very easy for that member to ignore his phone calls or emails. This is a defining feature of virtuality and wouldn't be possible in a collocated group. Another aspect of virtual leadership is the role of group members who are located closer to the customer than the leader. Facilitating their creativity and expertise is important for the company's overall success.

These are just some examples that show why classical leadership models fail in a global business setting. Dispersed groups require a different leadership model that includes the concept of Shared Leadership and is located between the poles of leader-centric and employee-centric (reverse management) leadership approaches.

Textbox 2.6: Definition: Dimension "Shared Leadership"

The degree to which all members proactively take responsibility for the overall success of the work of the group.

Item 1: The degree to which the individual roles and responsibilities are clear to members of the group.

This item addresses questions like: Do members know their own work-related roles in the group? Are members aware of the roles of other members in the group? Do members know their own responsibilities within the group? Are members aware of the responsibilities of other members within the group?

Item 2: The degree to which members proactively show responsibility for the overall success of the group.

This item addresses questions like: Is there a feeling of shared responsibility for the success of items driven and managed by other members? Do members proactively support other members regardless of roles and responsibilities if they think it is needed? If necessary, do members take responsibility for the tasks of other members, even if they are hierarchically higher or lower? Do members have the necessary overview of the work packages to become aware if support or substitution is needed?

Good Practice

Successful virtual collaboration requires a new perspective on leadership. Given the complexity of virtual group work, including the inability to be often together physically, leaders need to let go of control and hierarchy and rely on a different leadership strategy instead. Once a leader starts delegating responsibility to group members and these also accept that responsibility, then true cooperation and self-organization can happen. This is only possible, however, when each group member truly understands the what, when, and how of the project tasks and when the project status is continuously made transparent for everyone.

Giving and accepting feedback, i.e. voicing what is often critical, vitally depends on shared responsibility for the project.

Our Advice

With increasing workloads, many leaders have a tendency to control and plan more tightly, often causing their co-workers to become more passive rather than active. When leadership is shared in a group, tasks and responsibilities are delegated to members. In a diverse group, tasks can be delegated to culturally mixed tandems rather than to just one member. One example for Shared Leadership is rotating moderation in weekly (or monthly, etc.) meetings.

There is no standard recipe for Shared Leadership. The specific context and tasks will lead to an individually shaped practice. In the table below, we list five forms of Shared Leadership in virtual groups with increasing levels of self-organization and member empowerment[2]. We have complemented these five structures with examples from one of our clients, a global financial services enterprise.

Table 2.1: Shared Leadership Scenarios

Leadership structure	When to use
Permanent team leaders *Example: A new global and strategically very important project in a new market is started in a matrix organization. A very experienced group leader is allocated permanently to the group.*	• High degree of role differentiation among members • Members with different areas of expertise/ knowledge • Different areas of work tasks integrated by leader • High level of interaction between leader and individual members → Traditional and matrix organizations
Rotating team leaders *Example: A systems integration project has different phases that are all technology driven. All group members are very experienced in applying the different technological aspects. The different phases are led by rotating "topic champions" who have the greatest expertise in the respective phase.*	• Members perform similar tasks • Projects divided up based on client preferences and type of projects members enjoy • All members are equally able to lead. • All members know the particulars of the business. • Meetings are formally established • High level of trust • Some stable staff and procedures → Within a project, sub projects often have different priorities at different times. The experts for the specialized sub topics advance the whole project respectively. For the duration of their expert leadership, they become the leader of the whole group.

Leadership structure	When to use
Managing partners governing the overall operations in partnership with rotating project leaders who supervise specific projects or tasks.	• Diversified businesses; multiple projects for different companies • Members have distinct areas of expertise but can also support others • High level of trust • Comfortable with being leader or member → The corporate travel professional organizes the global travel system (i.e. internal bookings) of an organization by cooperating with independent partners in the respective business locations. She is responsible for the global quality management.
Facilitators or coordinators *Example: A new HR process developed in Germany is to be implemented in the North American business sites of an organization. The experienced local HR teams are responsible for the implementation in their locations. The German HR manager travels to the US to organize the kick off before the local HR groups take over. The German manager subsequently leads regular web conferences to support the self-organized local groups in critical situations.*	• Self-managing groups that need additional support • Open and constant communication and information exchange • Facilitators possess technical, interpersonal, and project- and task-management skills → Mature groups with very good self-organizing skills whose members have been working together for many years. They draw on external coaches or mentors for support.
Leaderless or self-led *Example: A recurring business process is implemented annually with just a few adaptations. A group has successfully implemented this process for the past five years. Everyone in the group clearly knows what to do when and in which quality. The group has been together for quite a long time. The current leader decides to hand the implementation over to the self-organized group.*	• Members with similar or equal status or rank • Members with similar backgrounds and expertise levels • Members choose to be part of a group that benefits them in some way and all are equally invested in the team's outcomes • High levels of trust → Experience exchange networks

2.7 Self Reflection: Lessons Learned from Chapter Two: "The First Encounter": Finding and Applying VPI Dimensions in the Story

In this part of Chapter Two, and in the corresponding parts of chapters Three, Four, and Five, we provide you with a guided tour to reflect potential learning about Inclusion and the corresponding four dimensions (Communication Styles, Work Styles, Feedback Competence, and Shared Leadership), based on elements of our story.

Communication Styles

You may recall that, in the preparation of the team's first virtual meeting, Bell deems himself to be structured and thorough: *Next to a glass of water, Bell has put his notes about the members of the circle to help him structure the meeting and "meet the participants where they are". This seems particularly important given that the choice of "team" members has not only been explicitly cross-cultural but also cross-functional in order to ensure representation of multiple perspectives.*

If Bell had taken his notes seriously, he might have guessed that the diversity of the new team members might also call for a variety of Communication Styles.

> Consider for a moment: What does this tell us about potentially diverse Communication Styles? What would you do to accommodate those needs before or during the meeting?

A good hint in that direction is Gupta's SMS: *Before the meeting starts, Bell receives an SMS from Gupta who congratulates him on being appointed leader of the Quality Circle: "Please accept my heartfelt congratulations. Can we speak after the meeting? Rgds Ranjit".*

Work Styles

Upon reading Ranjit's text, *Bell decides to reply later because he wants to concentrate on the meeting for now.*

Consider for a moment: What does this sentence reveal to us in terms of Work Styles?

Here it becomes obvious that Bell neither welcomes nor prefers handling several actions simultaneously. While we need to be careful to ascribe specific behaviour to any cultural group, German Work Styles often show a preference for working on one item at a time.

Differences in Work Styles also surface in Bell's preparation for the meeting. *Bell sent out a slide with the meeting agenda to all participants prior to the meeting.*

- *12:00 Welcome*
- *12:05 Introduction round*
- *12:15 First sharing of local practice*
- *12:45 Agree on project steps and time frame*
- *12:55 Action items*
- *13:00 Sign out*

Consider for a moment: What does this agenda reveal to us in terms of Work Style preference on Bell's part?

Bell shows an agenda-driven approach, while most Anglo-Saxons prefer an objective-driven approach to meetings by starting with the objectives and then agreeing on an agenda (if at all).

Feedback Competence

What was happening in the meeting? At the very beginning of the telephone conference, the following statement was made by Britt Svensson: *"Hey Florian, we need you to be more positive and motivational about our virtuality, especially since we should practice what we preach..."*

Consider for a moment: What does this statement reveal to us in terms of Feedback Competence?

This statement is a typical example for "voicing" within a group. Svensson addresses a key issue. The attitude of a leader towards the quality of the shared virtual collaboration space and the importance it plays in working together set the tone for virtual collaboration. If the attitude is deficit oriented ("the glass is half empty"), the attractiveness of this virtual space is diminished. An attitude that reflects using this virtual space as a resource to reach high performance ("the glass is half full") is contagious for group members in a positive way – an essential factor for creating a Purple Space.

Shared Leadership

Consider for a moment: Does Svensson's statement reveal a second VPI dimension?

Svensson also displays Shared Leadership by taking on the responsibility for improving the culture of collaboration.

Patricia Kennedy further displays Shared Leadership when she asks:

"Who, by the way, takes the minutes?" Bell answers immediately: "I've been keeping notes." Kennedy: "Great, Florian, but you don't need to do everything, let us know if you want someone to take over."

After having touched upon all four dimensions, we invite you to examine them even further by concentrating on Svensson's involvement. Please go through the following questions for reflection:

- How might Bell and the other group members perceive Svensson's communication style? What impact might this communication style have on the group's performance?
- How would you describe the leadership style Svensson has in mind when making this statement? Do you think that the other group members share this perspective? What impact could this have on the way Bell is perceived and accepted as a leader by the different group members?
- To what kind of working style could Svensson be alluding with her statement? What could be the impact of this working style on the group's performance?
- How would you describe Svensson's Feedback Competence and its impact on both the leader and the group?

After having analyzed the facets of the four dimensions of Inclusion in at least one example, we invite you to continue screening the story for further clues on Communication Styles, Work Styles, Feedback Competence, and Shared Leadership.

Having collected more "data", imagine being the leader of this group or an external consultant and ask yourself the following questions:

> What would you like to improve and why?
> What could be a measure to improve the virtual performance of this group?
> How would you bring the topic(s) into the group?
> How would you work on it/them?
> How would you monitor it/them?
> How would you keep the topic(s) alive?

Your Notes

2.8 Coaching Questions for Inclusion

Start with the following questions:

- What is your understanding of the category "Inclusion"?
- How would you describe the present situation in the group?
- Could you please describe what has been done so far to include the members?
- How do you think that the members would describe the group?
- How often does your group connect?
- What are your "hopes/wishes/plans" for the group in the future?

Communication Styles

- Please describe the present style of communication in the group.
- Do you have the feeling that it is easy for every member to understand other members?
- What do you think the members would say about your Communication Style?
- Can you see or feel any differences in the way of communicating?
- How do you think that the cultural background has an impact on the Communication Style of the members?
- Which examples illustrate that?
- What does good communication look like (from your perspective)?
- Does the group talk openly about the different styles?
- If you could decide, how would you like the communication to be?
- Do you use different ways of communicating proactively?

Work Styles

- Please describe the present style of working in the group.
- Do you have the feeling that it is easy to work together?
- How do you think the members would describe your way of working?
- Can you see or feel any differences in the Work Styles?
- How do you think the cultural background influence the Work Style(s) of the members?
- What examples do you have for that?
- What does a good Work Style look like (from your perspective)?

- Does the group talk openly about different styles?
- If you could decide, what would you like the work style to look like?
- Do you use differences in Work Styles proactively?

Feedback Competence

- What are you own experiences with feedback?
- When do you believe feedback is necessary?
- In which areas do you think feedback is beneficial and in which areas not?
- How is the feedback practised in the group at the moment?
- Who gives feedback to whom?
- Could you please give examples of feedback that has happened in the group?
- How often is feedback given?
- How do you think that the team members experience the feedback behaviour in the group?
- Do you, as a group, have a clear and shared view on feedback?

Shared Leadership

- What is your understanding of the dimension "Shared Leadership"?
- Do you experience, see, or feel that this is happing in your group at the moment?
- Please describe situations in the group where (from your point of view) Shared Leadership happened.
- Please describe situations in the group where (from your point of view) Shared Leadership was missing.
- "A good leader is…" – please describe your own expectations towards good leadership.
- "A good leader is…" – how do you think would the group members describe a good leader?
- How does the group handle critical situations at the moment?

Notes

1 Lewis, Myrna: Inside the No, http://www.deep-democracy.net.
2 Nemiro (1997, 2004).

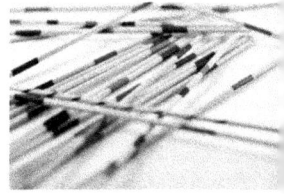

Organization and Process

3.1 The Story: A challenge in Chennai

3.2 The Four Dimensions of Organization and Process

3.3 Access to Information and Power

3.4 Workflow Integration

3.5 Organizational Relevance

3.6 Self-Organization Skills

3.7 Self Reflection: Lessons Learned from Chapter Three

3.8 Coaching Questions for Organization and Process

3.1 The Story: A Challenge in Chennai

Gupta asks the driver to take the coastal highway to avoid the traffic in the city centre. At this time of day – in fact, at any time except for the quieter hours between midnight and dawn – cars crawl through the city bumper to bumper.

He loves his home town, Chennai, and missed it dearly while studying at Harvard and working in Boston afterwards. But during the past few years, the infrastructural problems have grown. The return trip by car between Mylapor and the new headquarters located southeast of the airport now takes three hours – much too long.

Just when a bottleneck disrupts traffic completely, he sees an incoming call from Britt Svensson, his Swedish colleague from the "Global Virtual Quality Circle", within which they started working together a month ago. Despite closed windows he needs to speak very loudly in order to feel that his voice is audible in Sweden.

"Britt, what a pleasant surprise, how are you so early this morning in Sweden?"

"Thank you, Ranjit, I am fine. How about yourself? Your background sounds like a hornet's nest."

"Well, that is the Madras traffic, I am afraid. Have you been to Tamil Nadu yet?"

"I am afraid I never have, nor have I been to India, I must admit. But we could suggest to Moser and the team to have our face-to-face meeting there."

"Well, you would, of course, always be welcome. What gives me the honour of your call?"

"Well, since you are our IT guy and so internationally experienced, I briefly wanted to tap your Indian wisdom regarding a topic I see developing in our team."

"Well, my curiosity is wide awake."

"What I can see is that we made nice progress in our team's Workflow Integration, also thanks to your guidance. We are now all able to access the same data, which really makes a big difference. This would, of course, be a major asset if we could establish that for all global teams at Beltronik."

"Yes, absolutely."

"So the stage has been nicely prepared, but what I am noticing is that two players are not as present as the score calls for: there is very little coming from China and you are also a little slow in living up to the action items you have committed to."

"Ah, Britt, this is something that I have started to learn from you in these past weeks. While in the beginning I was quite shocked by the frankness of your feedback, I am beginning to appreciate it more and more. After all these years in India and the US, I am more used to expressing matters indirectly, if at all. And what I also appreciate is that we cannot wait for our team lead to address these issues, but should also take initiative ourselves. Be it as it may, your observation is correct: I have been slow in working off my action items. I simply have too much on my plate. With my regular workload, I already have a 10-hour day. Our team adds another one, if not two. And quite frankly, it is not on the top of my agenda because I don't think our project gives enough in return yet."

"What do you mean?"

"Well, I think they are cooking up something between Munich and Dubai and we only have the cheap seats at the table. Florian throws us a crumb or two every once in a while, but that is just not enough for me. I have been in this company for a decade and I would expect more, especially since India is always heralded as the future. And, quite frankly, it is also hard to convince my superior to invest more time in this project."

"Have you spoken with Florian about this?"

"Well, I dropped some hints, but I'll probably need to be more Swedish about it."

"Don't get us wrong. We're usually very tactful in our feedback. I tend to be viewed as confrontational here as well. What do you think about Florian?"

"Well, as long as this stays off the record: I like him a lot. He brings in a lot of enthusiasm, but also a lack of experience and seniority. During our kick-off call, for example, he embarrassed Yuan publicly by insisting on answers from him when it was clear that Yuan didn't have any. He also did not bring in Sakamoto-san the way he deserved. And he came up with an agenda without discussing it with us first and asking us for our objectives."

"I am glad you share this Pan-Asian perspective with me, because I did not notice either of the first two issues you mentioned."

"And there's something else: Yuan's slowness most likely has a lot to do with how our project has been sold to Shanghai. I doubt whether Moser has really rallied for the cause with Yuan's boss. If he does not get him onto it, we'll continue to have very slow reactions from Yuan, because he'll be busy with other stuff that seems much more relevant to him since it is relevant to his SUPERIOR."

"But I had the feeling that Yuan was interested in the matter. He's not a marionette, after all. He has a mouth, he could speak out."

"Britt, while I in India have a ten-hour day and another three commuting, I am a senior manager and can call my own shots up to a certain point. Yuan most likely cannot. And I hear that the work load in Shanghai is much harsher than here."

"I think one of the most important words we need to learn to pronounce in this company, no matter where we are in the organizational chart or on the map, is STOP."

"Well, so much for the quality-of-life orientation of you Swedes. Were you not the one that was on the cell phone while driving your children around?"

"Right, Ranjit: that is because I need to answer calls from you or other charming gentlemen."

Shortly after they hang up, traffic – that honking stream of sheet, rubber, men, and animals – starts moving again. Until not too long ago, elephants used to participate in Chennai's traffic, too. He remembers having a superior view of the city traffic while passing the Fort in Georgetown on horseback on a Sunday with his two daughters and his son.

Shilpa, Smita, and Suresh have reached an age at which their future would need to be decided. The search for suitable fiancés for all three and the wedding preparations for the girls would require a high time investment over the next two years. In addition, finding a job for Suresh, who had just finished his MBA at Harvard and returned to Chennai, will take some effort on Ranjit's part. And then, being the firstborn son, there is his responsibility to look after his parents' and siblings' wellbeing. His Swedish colleague would probably not understand the significance of these duties. In these matters, there would be no "STOP".

3.2 The Four Dimensions of Organization and Process

This category features dimensions that explore the organizational conditions and work processes influencing virtual performance.

Organization and Process is about the organizational embedding of a virtual group's work. Here, we seek to examine the quality of interaction between the organization and the virtual group. Both macro- and micro-organizational structures are of importance because the individual employee is the mirror of the organization as a whole. High virtual performance will flourish only under adequate institutional conditions. Individual ability to perform really well is intrinsically linked to the *Organizational Relevance* of a person's or a group's work. Unless a group is given *Access to Information and Power* necessary to fulfil organizational objectives, it won't be able to identify the critical factors for doing a good job. This also requires a high level of *Workflow Integration*, allowing work processes to flow smoothly through the organizational stream. Navigating organizational processes and preventing information and work overload demand high levels of *Self-Organization Skills* from individuals. From a psychological angle, this category is therefore also concerned with individuals finding a healthy way of dealing with their work, deciding which aspects they do or do not engage with.

> ➤ Think of navigating the work processes of a (virtual) group within an organization as being like riding a train across Europe. A meaningful, efficient, and enjoyable ride will be one in a fast train, on the main track, with the fewest possible disruptions and connections.

Riding a slow train on a side track and having to catch a different train at every border, on the contrary, would be tiresome, costing the traveller much time and energy. An integrated cross-border railway system is therefore beneficial for administrators and travellers alike. That is a system wherein top management will readily share relevant information and take necessary decisions in good time. But of course, international travel can be hard on some people. Handling the complexity of rapidly crossing time zones, borders, and cultures requires the ability and confidence to cope with such change.

3.3 Access to Information and Power

Most people want to be very close to the main lifelines of an organization or a community. When they achieve that closeness they feel that they are part of an "in-group". Feeling the pulse of an organization helps to make better and faster entrepreneurial decisions. Further, being seen and supported by top management provides the framework for high commitment and identification with the organization and the work. Here is our approach to operationalizing these ideas.

Textbox 3.1: Definition: Dimension "Access to Information and Power"

The degree to which members or a representative core group are involved in mission-critical communication and have management attention.

Item 1: The degree to which members of the group have direct access to information that is critical to the long-term context of the group's objectives.

This item addresses questions like: Are members involved in information and communication exchanges between the group and the organization that seem vital to the group's success? Do members – or at least some of them – communicate with the rest of the organization, customers, and decisions makers? Are members involved when important topics are addressed and critical decisions communicated?

Item 2: The degree to which the group's objectives have top management attention (Board, CEO, two levels higher than your direct report).

This item addresses questions like: Is senior management aware of the group's activities? Does senior management show interest in the project activities and status? Does senior management proactively support the group in achieving its objectives?

Good Practice

Global visibility and acknowledgement by top management are key for the success of a global project and for overcoming local "silo" thinking. Thus group leaders and members alike should market the importance of the group's contribution to the success of the organization and spread the news about current achievements. This can be done using organizations' formal communication channels as well as informal social networks. Attractiveness as an argument is crucial for securing necessary resources and management attention.

This also applies to information. Information is knowledge, and knowledge is power. Good organizing and processing as well as commitment are therefore dependent on the quality of information flows within an organization. Are employees given access to information and, by extension, to power? Are they provided with all the information relevant to their work? Are there media ruptures in the flow of information and work?

It often happens that one part of a group is closer to centres of information and power than others. In that case, information has to be shared with the more distant members in order to create Virtual Closeness. In this context, the leader of a team, and taking Shared Leadership into account also the members of the team, have different possibilities to close this informational gap.

Our Advice

A leader can forge Virtual Closeness with distant group members by starting virtual synchronous meetings with a round of sharing current developments and latest news from the company and/or local HQ – the power centre. When this is done informally (off protocol), such information is perceived as first-hand knowledge to which externals have no access. This can be a useful approach when working with group members from cultures that are exception-oriented rather than rule-oriented and prefer personal oral to formal written communication.

Information and power sharing is also achieved when distant members are included in local face-to-face meetings by putting up their picture on the desk or table. During all discussion and decision processes, the group stops at the picture and asks, what does this mean to our remote colleague? Is this information relevant for her or him? The result of these reflections can be shared in a running chat that is used to create the meeting minutes in real time. The remote colleagues may or may not be there, or have the option to read the chat protocol at any time or even react to the content in the chat. This way, they are included.

Yet another option is to invite top management representatives to a phone conference or any kind of web conference, or to set up a discussion forum where pressing questions of the group will be answered by the top managers and facilitated by the group leader or group members. This way, remote group members gain direct access to information from the decision makers themselves.

3.4 Workflow Integration

Even in the age of SAP we often encounter the following situation. There are different versions and levels of implementation of performance support systems – for example, controlling systems – throughout an organization. While some members located close to headquarters only need to press a button in order to get certain data, others in other locations have to export an Excel list from the system and calculate the same figures manually. In the words of the train example above, they have to switch trains and carry their luggage from one train to the other in order to reach their final destination. This can create a lot of frustration. Smooth and complete Workflow Integration is therefore an important prerequisite for high performance. When the shared workflow exists on paper it is important that everyone has the same understanding of it. If it is supported by IT systems, the higher the IT-based integration, the better performance will get.

Textbox 3.2: Definition: Dimension "Workflow Integration"

The degree to which members share the same workflow management system or work-relevant processes.

Item 1: The degree to which work processes are supported by a previously defined workflow management.

This item addresses questions like: Are most processes in the group supported by relevant workflow management systems? Are there varying degrees to which certain processes are defined and/or supported by workflow systems? Are processes connecting the group and the organization/customers/key players supported by workflow systems? Is there genuine support that creates trust in the workflow system?

Item 2: The degree to which members use the same previously defined workflow management.

This item addresses questions like: Does everybody have the same access to databases and workflow management systems? Do members actively use the workflow systems? Or do some members use tools or systems they believe are better suited? Do members instruct others proactively on areas of use that are new or foreign to them? Is there a continuous improvement process with respect to the workflow management system?

Good Practice

A workflow is integrated when it reduces the complexity of the shared working processes (who does what and when?) and managed consistently across programs, projects, organizational borders, and the corresponding interfaces. This may sound basic but it often presents a hot spot for conflict. Ideally, an organization enables barrier-free workflows back and forth within a team, group, or network and to their interfaces inside the organization. It finds out what kind of structure and also flexibility a virtual group needs in order to be high performing over the distance and makes it available. This can mean providing appropriate workspace or necessary technology and also avoiding stifling, overly bureaucratic reporting structures, or long response times.

Our Advice

Most importantly, organizations must design a common, global work-flow management system with standardized input and output steps that is used by all members consistently across the organization. This is a major part of the structure of a shared Purple Space. Ideally, the different stakeholders are involved in the setup phase of such a system.

> ➢ Once we were invited by a project-driven company to facilitate the process of setting up a global project-management system. The stakeholders in the different regions (Mexico, Germany, UK, Eastern Europe and others) were invited to jointly create the under-lying processes using a process mapping system. This became the basis for the business blueprint that was later realized and imple-mented by a global IT solutions company. The group worked together face-to-face for a whole month (!) before they went to their respective regions to discuss the results with their colleagues. They then returned for another period of consolidating the results. It was great to see how the different cultures had a different view on how flexible or how detailed the structuring of the processes should be. However, we were able to facilitate a consensus that wasn't based on one dominating culture.

Ruptures must be met with an inbuilt flexibility to improvise. Regular feedback and reviews to optimize the workflow management system in terms of processes, tools, and behaviours are crucial in order to strike a good balance between structural standards and flexibility.

Collaborative processes need to be transparent and visible for all group members. In more structured organizations, collaborative processes within a group are defined and supported by tools avail-able to all. In network organizations, groups tend to agree on dynamic regulations for cooperation and have one virtual meeting spot/hub where each member stores and shares their work steps in all updated versions. Regardless of the organizational type, it is important that all members understand the position and meaning of their own and their colleagues' contributions.

Also, the interfaces between groups within an organization must be managed and made visible to external stakeholders. This can be through password-protected online areas to which only members have access in order to develop and discuss ideas or projects before sharing them with management and others. This could also mean that external stakeholders such as suppliers or customers have access to shared processes or data – a very good sign of high levels of Workflow Integration and customer orientation.

3.5 Organizational Relevance

Feeling and knowing that the work done by individuals and groups is an important contribution to the success of the organization (and society) makes people feel good about their workplace. Motivation is fuelled when one's work is seen and appreciated by others, especially by management and other important stakeholders. The best way for an organization to be appreciative is to provide employees with the resources they require to do their work. It is less about distributing singular rewards. These are very strong factors in building Virtual Closeness also on an abstract level.

Textbox 3.3: Definition: Dimension "Organizational Relevance"

The degree to which the group's objectives and work are acknowledged and supported by the organization.

Item 1: The degree to which the work delivered by the group receives feedback from key stakeholders.

This item addresses questions like: Do members know all relevant stakeholders? Do the stakeholders respond to the information delivered by the group? Is there a common organizational interest in bringing the group's work forward?

Item 2: The degree to which group members have the resources they need to achieve their objectives (allocated time, tools, decision-making competences, etc.).

This item addresses questions like: Does the group have all the resources it needs to achieve the objectives? Is the group empowered to take care of its work-related needs?

Good Practice

From an individual's perspective, the question whether her or his work is relevant to and appreciated by the organization is central to both individual and organizational health. It is vital that management make an effort to demonstrate interest in their members' contributions. In addition to providing all necessary resources, they need to be present and show their people that the outcomes of groups' work are important to the organization.

Our Advice

It is the group leader's task to assess which resources his or her group needs and to lobby top management to make them available. The basis for this is the principle of attractiveness. If the group and its objectives resonate with management, people want to be part of the success story, either because they want to feel like winners or push their careers. This cannot be achieved with a negative attitude and persistent complaining about any bad conditions the group is facing. Rather, people should offer services and create benefits for the interfaces and the organization, including stakeholders.

A leader also needs to help senior management to see and support the projects and processes of his group. In virtuality, it may be easier to include a top leader into a virtual conference rather than inviting them physically. If doable, regular face-to-face fireside chats with top management members are a great way for groups to share successes and difficulties, thus enhancing their visibility. Using social media and other web-based communication systems such as micro blogging, business-related videos, or web conferencing within a business community can significantly support the visibility of a group.

> ➢ We are supporting the development of a community of about 1,000 controllers from different sites of a global energy provider. Every second month, a web conference is held with members of top management or other important stakeholders concerning a hot topic relevant to the controllers' work. Local controllers meet face-to-face in the different locations to attend their remote colleagues'

presentations and are able to interact through the chat with the presenters. On a regular basis, a group or a site can initiate or organize the "blog" of the month with a topic that is related to their current work.

The relevance of a group's work also ought to be clear to stakeholders. A stakeholder analysis is an important tool for the visualization of the degree of Virtual Closeness or virtual distance between the group and key stakeholders, and to come up with interventions to increase Virtual Closeness. One such strategy is to regularly include a group in key stakeholders' processes and ask for feedback.

➢ The HR team of an international company is spread out globally. Members are located on every continent and are responsible for their local subsidiary. Senior management has decided to standardize HR internationally. As the HR team was not involved in the decision, it feels that it is of little relevance to the organization. The impending standardization has led members to lose motivation given that they are being forced to undergo change. Getting these team members back on board requires working with them to identify the benefits of standardizing, thereby creating the necessity and the urgency for the change process to make it a priority. The best way for the organization to do this is by delegating the responsibility for the changes to the local HR heads and entrusting them with the implementation of the transformations locally. By giving them the leverage necessary to negotiate and implement the change process in their respective locations and by avoiding the trap of micromanaging the change process centrally, the organization creates Shared Leadership.

Alternatively, the team as a whole can escalate the project when it finds that the project is of low priority to its members. Escalation means creating clarity and jointly thinking about the consequences of stopping the project. This will usually lead to an awareness of the relevance each member gives to the project. If an escalation process confirms an overall low priority among team members, they have two options. They can finish the project quickly by investing only minimal time and energy. Or they can stop the project. Regardless of the result, it is crucial that the entire team decides to escalate and goes through the escalation process together. Escalation does not imply creating chaos but rather, gaining clarity about the existing relevance of the project and members' commitment to it.

3.6 Self-Organization Skills

Shared Leadership and working in a Purple Space need a much higher level of Self-Organization Skills than working together face-to-face. Creating the feeling that one is on the steering side of things and not in a reactive "firefighting" mode and a state of excessive demand is key to Virtual Closeness. Two aspects especially help to create that feeling: the abilities to filter relevant information from the endless stream of data running through an organization; and to focus on the right tasks to strike a good balance between local and global interests.

Textbox 3.4: Definition: Dimension "Self-Organization Skills"

The degree to which members employ self-management and self-organization skills to manage work packages and group success.

Item 1: The degree to which members have well-developed self-management skills for coping with the workload and task priorities.

This item addresses questions like: Do members find the right balance between their activities, constantly checking and readjusting priorities? Do members differentiate between the urgent and the important? Are members able to say "no" and make realistic assessments of their resources? Do members support each other to prevent burnout?

Item 2: The degree to which members proactively change their working environment and habits to deal with challenges to achieve group objectives.

This item addresses questions like: Do members keep processes going without outside pressure? Do members proactively change their working environment and habits to improve performance?

Good Practice

Ultimately, how people are embedded in an organization, which also depends much on the extent to which they *want* to be embedded, is intimately linked to the individual's ability to cope with information and process requirements. Self-Organization Skills are fundamental to integrating and dealing with information, organization, and process effectively and to handling complexity. It can therefore be important to provide employees with relevant training on self-management and Self-Organization Skills. Leaders play an important role in this. By taking on the role of a coach and asking coaching questions leaders can help to improve the Self-Organization Skills of the group members. Such questions may include the following.

➢ Have you ever had to deal with an excess of demands?

➢ How did you cope in the concrete situation?

➢ What helped you deal with it?

➢ What lessons can you apply in the present situation?

The essential aspect here is learning to prioritize and deal with pressure. Any coaching should therefore focus on initiating and supporting the self-conscious reflection of a person's expectations of his or her work. The goal is to place responsibility where it belongs by identifying the right priorities and the corresponding level of detail. What is really necessary?

Our Advice

Perhaps most crucially, organizations must encourage their members to develop solid competences in dealing with the unknown. Being able to thrive in situations in which the outcome or possible reactions are unknown is an important prerequisite for flexible performance and for organizational health. One aspect of this is work–life balance. Members must learn to maintain their long-term health to preserve the self and the group. This includes the ability to set boundaries for one's workload and communicate them, rather than overload. It also demands the ability to filter relevant aspects from a constant flow of information and to set adequate priorities.

Self-organization also means acting proactively in favour of one's group and project instead of passively waiting for instructions and external impulses. Group members should proactively shape their work conditions to enable good cooperation with others. These conditions include work times, available technology, Media Competence, work locations, and communication behaviour. The latter is particularly crucial. Group members need to produce a reliable and continuous communications behaviour and communicate proactively if there are (perceived) communication gaps or other difficulties.

Self-organization further suggests a certain amount of flexibility to react to an ever-changing environment. "Agile" project-management skills will help with flexible planning.

Essentially, self-organization requires the ability to decide consciously, and on a daily basis, "Who can cope with being disappointed today?" The ability to prioritize and deal with pressure is absolutely essential: for example, when opening one's email inbox in the morning and knowing that there are usually more messages than one person can manage to reply to in one day. This decision becomes increasingly important with growing leadership responsibility. A manager must be able to focus, prioritize, and distinguish between what's truly significant and urgent and what is not – without the burden of a constant bad conscience. Time-management and project-planning skills are not sufficient for self-organization. What is needed in addition is the ability to make a conscious choice to say "No".

There are also media aspects involved in this dimension. A growing number of companies shift from information push technologies to information pull systems by slowly moving away from email (push) communication towards using wikis, social media, or dedicated group support systems (pull). Think of such pull systems as firesides around which group members meet. This significantly decreases the information overload created by email flooding (ccing) and is a crucial step in creating Purple Spaces.

3.7 Self Reflection: Lessons Learned from Chapter Three: "A Challenge in Chennai": Finding and Applying VPI Dimensions in the Story

In this part of Chapter Three, we provide you with a guided tour to reflect on potential learning about the category "Organization and Process" and its corresponding four dimensions (Access to Information and Power, Workflow Integration, Organizational Relevance, and Self-Organization Skills), based on elements of our story.

Workflow Integration

After the first virtual meeting, the group has made some progress to which Britt Svensson refers when she calls Ranjit Gupta in the middle of Chennai traffic."*What I can see is that we made nice progress in our team's Workflow Integration, also thanks to your guidance. We are now all able to access the same data, which really makes a big difference. Of course, it would be a major asset if we could establish that for all global teams at Beltronik.*"

Consider for a moment: Why is Workflow Integration an essential element for the development of Virtual Closeness?

What Svensson addresses is a central aspect of virtual performance. Ideally, believing in the shared work process and using the necessary tools can be a starting point for creating a joint Purple Space. It is also a prerequisite for nurturing trust in collaboration. While trust in international contexts has multiple connotations, it nevertheless often means equal access to data.

Even with Workflow Integration established, motivation does not come automatically – as we learn from Ranjit Gupta: *"I have been slow in working off my action items. I simply have too much on my plate. With my regular workload I already have a 10-hour day. Our team adds another one, if not two. And quite frankly, it is not on the top of my agenda because I don't think our project gives enough in return yet."*

Consider for a moment: Which dimension is implicitly mentioned here? How does it affect Ranjit Gupta's motivation and perhaps the performance of the whole team?

Access to Information and Power

Later, Gupta expresses something that is essential for successful virtual collaboration. If some or most members of a group do not feel that they have equal Access to Information and Power, their commitment is bound to drop. Gupta states this directly. *"Well, I think they are cooking up something between Munich and Dubai and we only have the cheap seats at the table. Florian throws us a crumb or two every once in a while, but that is just not enough for me. I have been in this company for a decade and I would expect more, especially since India is always heralded as the future. And, quite frankly, it is also hard to convince my superior to invest more time in this project."*

If you were the leader of this team, which next possible steps could you take to develop Virtual Closeness in this dimension, not only for Gupta but for all potential stakeholders?

Organizational Relevance

While Gupta complains about a lack of access to information and involvement in decision making from the Indian side, he also directly points at another important facet of Virtual Closeness. *"And there's something else: Yuan's slowness most likely has a lot to do with how our project has been sold to Shanghai. I doubt whether Moser has really rallied for the cause with Yuan's boss. If he does not get him onto it, we'll continue to have very slow reactions from Yuan, because he'll be busy with other stuff that seems much more relevant to him since it is relevant to his SUPERIOR."*

Which dimension is touched upon here? What potential consequences might come to light not only during but also before a major project or collaboration scenario with diverse stakeholders?

When group members, in this case Yuan, don't have the necessary resources and backing of their superiors, it is almost impossible to reach high levels of virtual performance. The Organizational Relevance of a project both determines and often depends on the buy-in of key stakeholders. While this is essential for all organizational contexts, it can be even more crucial in cultures marked by strong hierarchies – for example, in many Asian contexts. One important aspect of the whole group's performance could therefore be to empower Yuan by aligning his superior's needs with the objectives of the group.

Self-Organization Skills

Shortly before ending their phone conversation, Britt Svensson touches upon another aspect of Virtual Closeness: Self-Organization Skills: *"I think one of the most important words we need to learn to pronounce in this company, no matter where we are in the organizational chart or on the map, is STOP."*

Consider for a moment: How does this dimension affect the success of this particular group directly and indirectly? How does it affect virtual collaboration in general? What concrete steps can group leaders, and in the context of Shared Leadership also group members, take in order to enhance the development of Self-Organization Skills? Could there be organizational or national-cultural aspects that might make it more difficult to support Self-Organization Skills? What could one do in order to deal with these roadblocks?

After having analyzed the facets of the four dimensions of Organization and Process in at least one example, we invite you to continue screening the story for further clues on the dimensions of Access to Information and Power, Workflow Integration, Organizational Relevance, and Self-Organization Skills.

Having collected more "data", imagine being the leader of this group or an external consultant and ask yourself the following questions:

What would you like to improve and why?

What measure could be taken to improve the virtual performance of this group?

How would you bring the topic(s) into the group?

How would you work on it/them?

How would you monitor it/them?

How would you keep the topic(s) alive?

Your Notes

3.8 Coaching Questions for Organization and Process

Start with the following questions:

- What is your understanding of the category "Organization and Process"?
  (If needed, it would be good to give some input on "Organization and Process".)
- How would you describe the present situation in the group?
- Could you please describe how you are organized in the group?
- Which processes do you proactively use?
- Do all members have the same/all processes available?
- If you could choose, which processes would you like to implement in the group?
- How do you think that the members would describe the situation?
- What are your "hopes/wishes/plans" for the group in the future?

Access to Information and Power

- Do you share information with all members?
- Which information do you share with which members?
- What could happen if you shared even more information with the members?
- What do you as a leader need in order to feel more comfortable in sharing important information with the group?
- What do you as a leader need in order to feel more comfortable in sharing critical decisions with the group?
- What could happen if you did share more?

Workflow Integration

- How does the work flow between the members and the locations?
- If you could decide, what would you like the flow to look like?
- Please explain what makes it difficult to share the same workflow/processes?
- What is needed to change that?
- Who would be the key players you need to change the situation?

- Which kind of support from the members do you need in this process?

Organizational Relevance

- Please describe the relevance of the project/topic to the organization.
- Would it be possible to gain more attention in the organization for the work/objective of your group?
- Who in the organization would it be important to win over as a supporter?
- What would be the necessary actions to take?

Self-Organization Skills

- Please go through the following for each member:
- How self-organized is this member?
- What would be needed from your side to support this member to become more self-organized?
- What would be needed from an external side to support this member to become more self-organized?

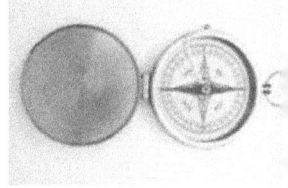

Space and Time

4.1   The Story: Connection Atlanta – Paulista

4.2   The Four Dimensions of Space and Time

4.3   Geographic Advantage

4.4   Work Schedule Overlap

4.5   Time in Shared Dialogue

4.6   Time Investment

4.7   Self Reflection: Lessons Learned from Chapter Four

4.8   Coaching Questions for Space and Time

4.1 The Story: Connection Atlanta – Paulista

Paolo's Story

Paolo steps out of the elevator that took him from the underground parking lot to the first floor. He is still surprised how classy this new "JK Iguatemi" is compared to other malls that have been built throughout the country. In Brazil, shopping, like soap operas, has become the favoured focus of social interaction and this mall is clearly the most luxurious of all.

The same is true for their new apartment in Jardims, below Avenida Paulista. The neighbourhood has become even more expensive since global enterprises stopped believing, a few years ago, that Latin America could be run from Miami. Hundreds of companies have flocked to Sao Paulo since then. The price per square meter has exploded in the upscale neighbourhoods. The situation would be laughable were it not that serious.

Unlike Paolo, Ivete, his wife, is a real Paulistana. Her parents always lived in Paraìso, the district neighbouring Jardim. Beltronik has been in town since 1972, with head-quarters in Higionopolis, a neighbourhood that has since become part of the city centre. It would therefore be crazy to move house to Alphaville or any of the other suburbs given that he could cycle to work from his current house, if he knew how to cycle.

This thought reminds him of his mission: he is supposed to get his son Fabio a moun-tain bike for his birthday. He knows that Fabio will never ride the bike but since his stinking-rich peers all own mountain bikes, the family has to go along and get him one, too. White with Shimano gear shifters. Many of his old friends from university believe that hot Paolo has made it – the lucrative position with Beltronik, the apart-ment in Jardims, beautiful Ivete – and his son attends the same birthday parties as Ronaldo's son. But none of his middle-class friends can really understand the enor-mous financial and social efforts necessary to have all of this.

That is why his career at Beltronik is so important. It is a stepping stone to a more superior social position. Salaries in Brazil are currently leaping forward. Proving himself in the Global Virtual Quality Circle would accelerate his career development, at Beltronik and elsewhere. He would finally be able to stop worrying about loans and start living.

But in his own view, Paolo has been rather cut off from the project so far. It has been virtually impossible to build a relationship with the East Asians. Only Ranjit seems to be open and available. He also feels that he and the US American woman aren't really included, probably because they are located in the wrong time zone.

Before entering the bike store, he redials Patricia Kennedy's number for the third time that evening. Again only her voicemail answers, "This is Pat, leave a message, beep". The tone of this message sounds as cool as her emails, which often only consist of one or two lines without salutation or closing. How to discuss improving virtual collaboration when even the most basic things like politeness are rationalized?

Patricia's Story

For two years now, Patricia has been making the trip from her mother's nursing home in Forest Park up to Decatur. Many of her friends have asked her why she won't move to a nicer area. But she grew up here, danced with the soul sisters to the Commodores' songs in front of the mirror; her church is here, she belongs here.

She is still grateful that Beltronik, after the many years she worked with them in Germany, has agreed to relocate her position as Vice President of Global HR from its headquarters in Munich to the insignificant Atlanta location. The US headquarters in L.A. would have been a more respectable choice but it is too far from her ill mother. Besides, in L.A. she would be operating from a fringe time zone and that would be very detrimental to her global responsibility. In Atlanta, the time-zone issue is reduced by three hours and Hartsfield-Jackson airport, in addition to offering excellent international connections for her one-hundred-plus travel days per year, neighbours Forest Park.

She looks at her display. During the three hours she spent with her mother she received 69 emails and 22 messages. Three messages are from Paolo Azevedo in Brazil who has been trying to reach her for days – a nice but inexperienced and complicated guy who is "full of himself". His emails are full of empty phrases and it costs her quite an effort even to open them. The last email from him that she read had 28 lines! She can't remember ever having written such a long a letter. While traffic on Highway 285 North is becoming heavier, she calls Paolo back.

The Americas

"Boa tarde. Que coisa, it's you, Patricia. I really appreciate you calling me back at this hour."

"No sweat, Paolo. I'm in the middle of slow traffic and I figured this would be the right time to pass you the medal for outstanding patience."

"Uhm, I'm sorry Patricia, what do you mean?"

"It was a lame joke, Paolo, forget it. You called several times and I am aware that I still owe you a couple of mails, so I figured it's time for me to act as a responsible member of the Global Virtual Quality Circle."

"Oh yes, thank you. So how have you been?"

"Fine, Paolo, just fine. How about yourself?"

"Fantastic, thank you. What I meant to speak with you about is our situation."

"Which one are you referring to?"

"Us as Americans."

"You mean North and South?"

"Yes."

"So?"

"Well, haven't you noticed we are sort of cut off from the rest of the team?"

"What do you mean?"

"Well, Munich has it really easy. They sit right in the middle of the map and can communicate with the rest of the world over lunch. But we are at the edges and I think they keep on forgetting us."

"Evidence?"

"Well, first of all Florian always invites with Munich time. I think it would be considerate to mention our time zones in the invitation as well."

"Point taken."

"And they usually schedule our meetings in a way that the Asians can still attend at reasonable hours – you know that the Japanese often work until eight at night – while we need to get up at unholy hours. My wife already hates me for it."

"I'm getting it. It's a conspiracy against America."

"Quit joking, Patricia. What's your real perspective on this?"

"No, I couldn't agree more. But I sort of volunteered for this time zone when I applied for a transfer back from Germany, so who am I to complain?"

"Entendo. But if we're supposed to be a task force exploring the best virtual practice, as Florian says, then we need to approach this differently. We're also losing out on the work packages…"

"Go on…"

"Pois, when we were supposed to all work together on the first presentation to board, we moved in the wrong direction."

"Meaning?"

"Ever heard of follow-the-sun?"

"You're right, coming to think of it. We were pressed for time and did not really manage a relay, since we started in Munich and not here."

"Isso!"

"And we didn't really get to include our inputs because Florian still wanted his assistant to go over it before it was show time for the board."

"I felt cheated. And I feel left out now. My work is not recognized as much as it deserves. Should Florian one day be asked to evaluate my performance, he has no clue. And I think others invest far less than I do. From Yuan, for example, we get almost nothing."

"Don't take it too personal."

"Patricia?"

"Alright, I agree, we need to ring the bell. And we definitely need to spend more time in communication if we want to establish best practice in this company."

"Great. Shall I draft a mail from both of us?"

"Paolo?"

"Yes?"

"Trust me. You want to leave this to Patti."

4.2 The Four Dimensions of Space and Time

This category features the decisive dimensions in the framework of geographical locations and time zones that influence virtual performance.

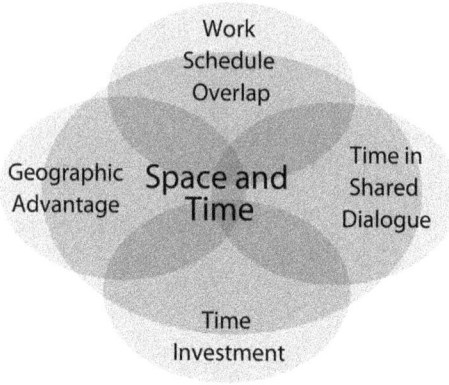

Work
Schedule
Overlap

Geographic
Advantage **Space and Time**

Time in
Shared
Dialogue

Time
Investment

One of the defining characteristics of virtuality is that *Space and Time* are disconnected in the reality of remote collaboration. With group members dispersed around the globe in different time zones, organizations have the *Geographic Advantage* of being closer to customers, decision makers within the organization, and business partners in the respective locations. Some groups allow their members to work from private, favoured locations like a cottage in Tuscany or a Texan hacienda, for example.

However, working across different time zones also reduces common work-time slots for all group members, often resulting in a low *Work Schedule Overlap* and the respective need for management. "Out of sight" often also leads to "out of mind" and consequently to lower *Time Investment* into virtual group work. In order to transform these challenges into opportunities for increased performance, the goal is to find strategies for coping with the disconnection of time and space. By helping groups to create and use *Time Shared in Dialogue* productively, space and time can be reconnected and Virtual Closeness is built.

When working with virtual groups, the focus in this category is on creating synchronous time for a regular shared dialogue – the so-called *heartbeat*[1] of a group (asynchronous communication will be covered in Chapter Six). Suppose that virtual group members can invest 20 per cent of their work time into a global project. If they don't spend a significant amount of that time in synchronous work to keep track of the status, current decisions, and demands of the project, this 20 per cent is not being used as effectively as it could be. It is therefore crucial that group members are given sufficient time for a global project[2] and that, according to the tenets of agile project management, they spend that time in as much synchronous collaboration as needed. This requires them to create a substantial amount of Work Schedule Overlap. Performance starts to increase significantly once groups agree on how to use their time together – which also marks a major contribution to creating the Purple Space-time.

> Imagine the world as a functional, flexible puzzle. The pieces represent shared Time and Space that easily fit together in their local systems. When a global system is created, however, pieces will be taken out of their local contexts and placed so as to invest time into virtual teamwork. Members in different locations and/or time zones float through the organization on separate puzzle pieces of Time and Space. The challenge is to assemble the pieces into a coherent picture of a dialogue in shared time that makes sense to all. That way, a new, virtual puzzle emerges through the time groups spend in shared dialogue.

> Imagine a member of a global virtual group, who works on several projects at the same time, entering a different office for each separate project. If she is part of seven projects in seven offices and one of the projects is virtual, she will go to the virtual office whenever she intends to work on the virtual project. If there is not enough Work Schedule Overlap with her far-flung colleagues, that office will often be empty when she enters (because the others are not online). Chances are high that she will leave the empty office much more quickly than she would if her colleagues were there at the same time. (Similarly, in asynchronous settings, she will likely leave if her co-workers leave no traces – see Chapter Six.) In virtuality,

that office space could be the Purple Space, which needs to be filled with closeness and performance by all members. Members actually need to show up, be there together at the same time, and leave traces in order to fill the Purple Space with life. For this, they need to create enough overlapping time in their work schedules to be in the room together. See the section Work Schedule Overlap, below, for advice on how to achieve this.

4.3 Geographic Advantage

Time zones are given as soon as the geographic dispersion of a group has been decided. Working across time zones is not an easy thing and often leads to diminishing performance. It is therefore essential that the dispersion of group members to different locations creates a significant benefit for the organization and the group. This section is dedicated to exploring how such benefits can be brought to an organization's awareness.

Textbox 4.1: Definition: Dimension "Geographic Advantage"

The degree to which members lever their geographic distribution to achieve their group objectives and optimize individual working conditions.

Item 1: The degree to which members are geographically close to key stakeholders/ customers.

This item addresses questions like: Are members aware of the proximity of customers to other team members and the possible advantages for their organizational and business objectives? Is it possible for some members to visit key customers and stakeholders within a few hours?

Item 2: The degree to which members can personally choose the place of their work location.

This item addresses questions like: Do members have a choice regarding their work location (travel, home, office, etc.) and do they act accordingly? Are they clear about the advantages of this location for their own lives and work? Can they convincingly communicate their location needs within the group? Are other members open to exploring the possibilities of shifting locations?

Good Practice

Geographic distribution is usually a conscious corporate choice, rather than a necessary evil. It is vital for an international enterprise to place its people as close to the different customer or stakeholder localities as possible. In fact, virtual groups are usually composed according to those needs, with the separation in time and in space consciously taken into account.

The corporate reasons for this are usually twofold. On the one hand, internationally operating organizations with subsidiaries in different locations want to provide the basis for global growth by standardizing values and operations. On the other hand, they often want to save costs by centralizing certain business operations such as human resources. Rather than having decentralized human resources departments in every location, it is more efficient to have a global HR head managing local HR specialists who implement standardized corporate policies in their respective locations.

Good practice also includes navigating the time zones involved according to the "follow the sun" principle. This allows groups to provide a given service continuously across time zones. It is always a great experience to surprise the customer with something that is dealt with while he or she is sleeping.

Our Advice

The benefit of dispersed groups is that their members are often located close to local customers and thus have a better and faster understanding of their context and needs. That way, a group can build physical closeness and offer its clients short response times as well as a high-intensity dialogue. Another benefit of global groups is that they are often a more cost-effective solution than local groups. It is therefore important for complex organizations to deconstruct their local groups in favour of global spreading when this is necessary and possible. The following image visualizes this deconstruction.

Figure 4.1: Local Deconstruction

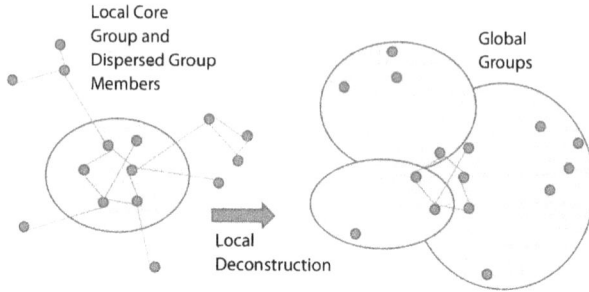

> One of our clients is a global group whose members work on two continents. The group was dealing with challenges in communication and collaboration in part because they did not perceive their geographical locations as advantageous for working together successfully. To promote their respective sites, the group members explored the hidden benefits of their locations and "sold" them to their colleagues. Through asking, "What makes our location interesting for colleagues in other locations? What is attractive about our location?", participants could appreciate, for example, the immense benefit of one part of the group being located in a global technology hub while the others were closer to important markets.

From the perspective of geographical distribution, it is easier to run a virtual group that is equally dispersed as opposed to one whose majority is located in one spot with a few single colleagues in remote spots.

> When joining an online meeting or a phone conference, the notion of someone being brought into the meeting is still widely spread. This presupposes one person, say a manager, who is responsible for bringing her group members into a phone or video conference with far-flung partners. For a collaboration space of reduced complexity and filled with closeness – the prerequisites of a Purple Space – however, it is vital that we think of participants as coming together in the common interaction space just as if they physically entered a meeting room. The manager (or the organization) provides and partly fills this space with a structure, thereby fulfilling a typical task of virtual leadership. Rather than being brought into the meeting by someone else, they join the shared Purple Space as equal participants – each and every one of them.

High group performance requires sufficient flexibility on the part of the organization. Part of this flexibility is to allow people to choose the place from which they work. When employees are encouraged to work from a place where they are very creative and inspired and have the necessary focus and concentration to deliver their work, their performance usually increases significantly. While this is widely accepted wisdom, many contemporary organizations still require their members to work in environments such as open-plan offices where the lack of private space may impede communication and creativity, not to mention the frequent interruptions by people approaching one's desk with "just a quick question..." and the noise of the surroundings.

4.4 Work Schedule Overlap

Within the time-zone restrictions that geographically dispersed groups face, the overlap of the different locations' working hours usually cannot be tweaked much. This overlap defines the maximum time that can be spent in shared synchronous dialogue. Nevertheless, there are more or less efficient ways of dealing with these restrictions. The following section offers suggestions for how to do that.

Textbox 4.2: Definition: Dimension "Work Schedule Overlap"

The degree to which members share overlapping work schedules proactively.

Item 1: The degree to which all members of the group can possibly work together at the same time.

This item addresses questions like: Are members working in different time zones? What are the possible overlapping working hours? How are members distributed across time zones to enable the transfer of work packages if needed?

Item 2: The degree to which members are flexible and able to change their working hours so that they could work as a group at the same time.

This item addresses questions like: Is information about time zones, public holidays, general local working hours and time adjustments (i.e. daylight saving) easily accessible to everybody? Are members willing and able to change their working hours flexibly in order to provide for a sufficient overlap? Do members, when organizing work packages and processes, plan the flow according to other members' schedules? Is this flexibility acknowledged and positively re-enforced by team members and leaders?

Good Practice

Creating adequate Work Schedule Overlap requires not only planning for virtual group time but also for physical encounters, when possible. Groups then need to decide how to use their time together in the most efficient way. As we will see in Chapter Six, there is much tested wisdom about how to design a virtual meeting and also how to make the best use of the time between meetings; for which tasks to best use it (or not); whether or not to plan for a collocated kick-off meeting; and so on. While finding Work Schedule Overlap is often perceived as a major challenge by spread-out groups, it is quickly mastered once Virtual Closeness is built.

The important thing is to create enough shared synchronous working time for all group members. That time, however, needn't be spent in dialogue with all members. Rather, members need to be able to reach each other during that time and should have the feeling that their colleagues are working towards the same goal, at the same time. This feeling can be created, for example, by seeing that the others are online or that documents are uploaded which, in turn, creates the feeling of Virtual Closeness – of being in the Purple Space at the same time.

> ➢ We wrote this book as a virtual group of co-authors. We are spread over three different cities across Germany, and most of us travel for work most of the time. While giving the chapters their final polish, we would often work at the same time (synchronously) at our respective offices. When there were questions or when we needed to discuss specific topics or share ideas, we could always call each other, albeit only for a short conversation. On some days, it was just to say, "Hi I see you are also online – good morning!" On other days, we didn't have questions and there was no need to be in dialogue. But we dedicated our energy towards the same project at the same time which was visible for all of us by way of notifications like "A new document has been uploaded" or "Line Jehle is online".

Our Advice

When agreeing on overlapping work time, groups tend to fall victim to national "egocentrism" and schedule in favour of the location where the majority of the members are. This may force remote colleagues to put in very early or very late hours on a regular basis, creating an imbalance that is not beneficial for Virtual Closeness. Distributing Work Schedule Overlap equally across time zones and rotating the commitment to log on during fringe times supports a fair balance within a group.

> ➤ When group members live in time zones that don't easily allow for shared time during working hours, weekly rotations are a good way of creating Work Schedule Overlap. Consider a virtual group with three members, Paul, Lisa, and Jose, who live in three different time zones. Paul invests 10 hours per week in the virtual project, Lisa invests 30 hours, and Jose invests 20 hours. To create time overlap efficiently, they agree to work together synchronously every Thursday. Thursdays are reserved for making decisions, discussing important matters, or solving conflict – things that are best done synchronously. In order to distribute the burden of working during fringe hours equally, they rotate on a weekly basis. That way, the workflow can also be better coordinated. Paul, for instance, will try to finish his part of the work before Wednesday, knowing that Lisa will take over on Thursday morning.

> ➤ A group that is spread across two time zones – the UK and the US, for example – agrees to reserve two hours in the afternoon or morning respectively for collaboration. The UK colleagues block their calendars from 3–5pm, the US colleagues during the corresponding morning hours, for simultaneous work on their project. Commitments in their respective local offices are not scheduled during those two hours. That way, regular Work Schedule Overlap is created and becomes embedded in the group's daily routines. If one of the members or even the entire local group happens not to be available during the agreed time, they will signal this in advance so the group can work around it.

In very challenging scenarios, where group members are spread to an extent that makes it more or less impossible to find overlapping time for all, those based in the "middle" may mediate between the locations that are too far apart. In global groups with members on at least three continents, European-based members will often take on this role. Another option is that two European group members are responsible for one respective time zone each (one for US-based colleagues and one for colleagues in East Asia). They will synchronize their communication during regular work hours and/or use an asynchronous documentation tool, such as a WIKI, to create the global picture.

Building a workflow that supports continuous performance across time zones is another useful instrument for global groups. Two elements are particularly important here. First, a smooth process of handing over work from one time zone to another will help to ensure seamless continuation of productivity. If the workflow system, for example, enables a US-based group to take over from their Asian colleagues when these end their working day, customer support is ensured around the clock. Also, a problem occurring late in the day in Asia may be solved by US colleagues while the Asian colleagues sleep, allowing them to return to a cleared scene the next morning. Second, relying on such a continuous workflow presupposes the necessary level of closeness between group members. If, in the above example, the Asian and US colleagues feel close to each other and to their collaboration space, they are much more likely to entrust the other side with a problematic scene and provide them with all required information to solve the issue. See Workflow Integration in Chapter Three for more information on creating an integrated workflow in virtual settings.

Time-zone calendars are another great tool for connecting spread-out group members with one another. The important context of the respective locations can be made visible, including information like the time it takes to travel to the office. Suddenly, the efforts remote colleagues need to make in order to participate in virtual communication outside of their office hours become tangible and can be considered more easily in planning phases.

Moreover, introducing flexible working hours can significantly improve Work Schedule Overlap.

It is crucial to understand that members can only increase their availability on a voluntary basis and that asking for additional Time Investment is a culturally sensitive issue. Therefore, the different existing expectations and possibilities in a diverse group need to be clear to all participants. The mere process of negotiating increased member presence while keeping results open can already lead to improved performance and strengthen the Purple Space.

In the following image, the colored lines denote the overlap of typical work hours (9am – 5pm) in 13 major cities. The corresponding lines in the clocks show the best time of day for having a global phone conference in the respective locations.

Figure 4.2: The Best Time

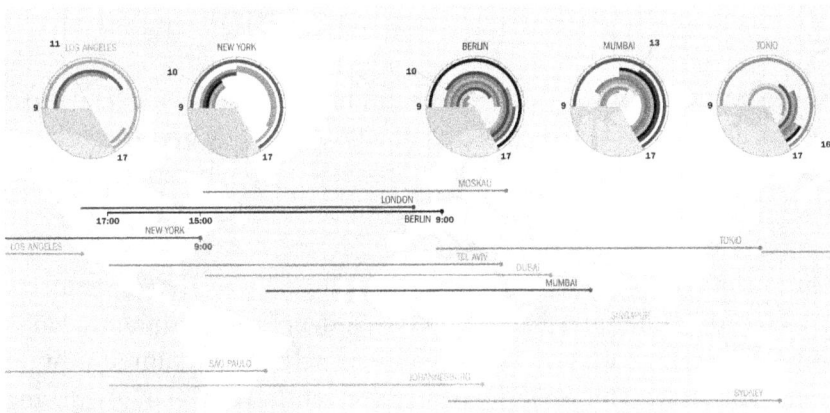

Adapted with permission from Segalla, M. and Sandner, K. (2010) Die globale Telefonkonferenz. Harvard Business Manager, November 2010, p. 2/3

4.5 Time Shared in Dialogue

Once a virtual group has realized its inherent Geographic Advantages and optimized its members' Work Schedule Overlap, it can proceed to fine-tuning its synchronous meetings – time in shared dialogue.

Textbox 4.3: Definition: Dimension "Time Shared in Dialogue"

The degree to which members see and/or hear each other at the same time.

Item 1: Amount of time members dedicate to simultaneous meetings when they can see or hear each other.

This item addresses questions like: Do I feel individual members have the same understanding of the importance of shared synchronous time? Do we put sufficient effort into making time for synchronous meetings when dealing with the demands of the organization(s)?

Item 2: Amount of time the group dedicates to simultaneous group meetings when they can see or hear each other.

This item addresses questions like: How much time does the group invest in synchronous meetings? Does the group as a whole understand the importance of making time for synchronous meetings? Do members exert their influence to ensure sufficient meeting time where all hear, see or read each other?

Good Practice

When working globally, spatial separation of group members almost always also means temporal separation. It is vital that groups work out how much time they need for synchronous communication and how they can use Work Schedule Overlap for shared dialogue.

Given that synchronous meetings with all group members require a lot of effort, finding a balance between synchronous (phone, video conference, web conference, etc.) and asynchronous communication (email, discussion forums, WIKI, etc.) is essential. Interestingly, having too many face-to-face or online meetings can lead to a decrease in performance. We all know the curious phenomenon of asynchronous dialogues breaking down right before face-to-face meetings because we are lured into thinking that, "we can sort this out when we meet face-to-face". Finding the right meeting frequency that fits a group's development speed and doesn't lead to a breakdown of asynchronous dialogue threads is an important leadership task. This frequency is called the heartbeat of a group[3].

Our Advice

The time spent in shared dialogue, both virtually and in person, creates a group's heartbeat. When sufficient virtual dialogue, using different media with different levels of media richness, is interspersed with regular face-to-face interaction, a group's heartbeat might resemble the one depicted below (with peaks indicating media richness).

Figure 4.3: Irregular Heartbeat of a Virtual Group

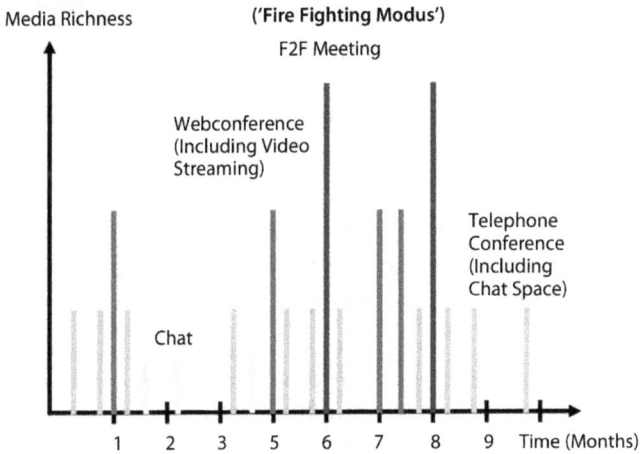

Adapted with permission from Maznevski, M., and Chudoba, K.M. (2000) Bridging space over time: Global virtual team dynamics and effectiveness. *Organization Science* 11(5): 473–92, Copyright 2000, the Institute for Operations Research and the Management Sciences, 5521 Research Park Drive, Suite 200, Catonsville, MD 21228.

This group:

- Meets face-to-face every six months for one-and-a-half days (with face-to-face being the richest medium),

- Has a two-hour phone or web conference including video streaming every two months (the latter being the medium with higher media richness), and

- Has a monthly chat.

Maznevski has suggested the following golden rule. If a group has a regular heartbeat, its productivity is generally higher than those of groups with irregular heartbeats. The latter are mostly in a "fire-fighting" modus, calling for an emergency meeting only when there is a crisis. Then everyone has to halt daily business to prepare for the meeting.

In the absence of a routine, the mode of friendly avoidance so easily used in virtuality can quickly lead to an irregular heartbeat. Once a rhythm is negotiated and established and commitment created, however, cancelling regular virtual meetings is no longer a convenient option. If a group member needs to be absent from a regular meeting, he will ask a colleague to take over his part (moderation, for example). Or he can react to questions or ideas in a chat forum in his own time.

No matter what types of communication a group agrees on, it is vital that they find a rhythm and adhere to it. This is a fundamental basis for a healthy heartbeat and for Virtual Closeness.

Synchronous communication, in particular, will benefit from a common meeting culture. High-quality online meetings can include the following elements that constitute the Purple Space:

- Purpose, agenda, and meeting goals that are identified by the meeting owner (possibly in dialogue with the group members – Shared Leadership!) and distributed well before the meeting to allow participants to prepare.

- The rotation of moderating and facilitating roles, including someone who watches the time.

- The keeping of a team clock to ensure that everyone speaks.

- The use of breaks after an hour or 90 minutes to avoid exhaustion.

- Provision of formal and informal communication and meeting spaces (channels) simultaneously to meet all cultural communication needs.

- Slowing down natives by asking them to write the meeting minutes during the meeting in real time (using a chat function).

In longer virtual meetings with a conference character and a higher number of participants, it is advisable to limit their total number to 12. The optimal number of participants in online meetings is six to eight – a size that allows everyone to speak. To get work done in an online meeting, it is therefore very useful to break up a larger group into smaller units of six to eight members and ask their representatives to present the results of their discussions to the panel later.

Using a rich variety of media is crucial for both synchronous and asynchronous communication modes. While a smooth asynchronous exchange depends on the availability of a variety of chatting and sharing functions, synchronous communication works well when using platforms that combine video, chatting, and file-sharing functions. It is also advisable always to provide a separate phone link in addition to video conferencing in case the latter isn't working (and vice versa).

(For more information on media and technology, see Chapter Eight.)

4.6 Time Investment

All the aspects discussed so far in this chapter will be obsolete if group members can't invest sufficient time in the virtual project, either because they are not allocated the necessary resources by their superiors or because of other work-related priorities. These issues of resource allocation and self-management appear as often in virtual collaboration as in traditional project management. However, having enough time and the will to invest this time in virtual collaboration is a major factor in creating Virtual Closeness.

Textbox 4.4: Definition: Dimension "Time Investment"

The degree to which members spend their work time on group objectives.

Item 1: Amount of time individual members invest to ensure achievement of objectives.

This item addresses questions like: After receiving a work package, do members invest enough time to accomplish the tasks? If there is an uneven distribution, do members feel that this makes sense under the given circumstances? Do members feel that other members have the same understanding of how much time should be spent on the different work packages?

Item 2: Amount of time the group invests to ensure achievement of objectives.

This item addresses questions like: Does the group allot enough time to ensure a successful completion of objectives?

Good Practice

A fundamental prerequisite for successful virtual collaboration is investing enough time in it to begin with. This is a leadership and expectation-management issue. Authentic personal commitment to Time Investment in virtual collaboration presupposes a virtual environment – a culture – wherein people want to participate, and feel appreciated for their diversity, valued for their work, and responsible for a shared process towards a shared goal. These aspects shape the Purple Space.

Our Advice

Every individual has personal preferences regarding the lowest and highest amount of time spent working directly with others. Remember the study by Cummings and Haas (2012) wherein they show that, when group members invest less than 40 per cent of their time in common work, there is no significant feeling of attachment between the group and the member. That feeling of attachment describes well our concept of Virtual Closeness. Conversely, continuous and significant Time Investment defines the "core" of a group.

In our organization-development practice, we often encounter groups that show team characteristics (the core group invests 40 per cent of their capacity) as well as network characteristics (members who join a group on a task-by-task basis or who invest less than 40 per cent in the group).

Figure 4.4: Group with Team and Network Characteristics

Group with team and network characteristics:
Core group with members who have 40% capacity for the
group work and group members outsideof the core with
less capacity for the group work

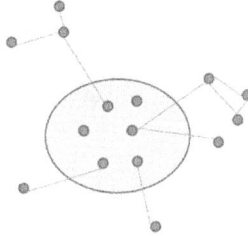

When setting up a virtual group, it is therefore crucial to include enough people who are willing to dedicate at least 40 per cent of their time to group activities and communicative processes. One of the main management tasks of virtual leaders is to negotiate this commitment with the leaders of the respective group members' locations.

When some members cannot invest the necessary time, a leadership decision is in order. They will either need to leave the project; or the time they can invest needs to be bundled and sold as limited expert time. Those group members should be regarded as a network around the core group and expectations adapted accordingly.

4.7 Self Reflection: Lessons Learned from Chapter Four: "Connection Atlanta – Paulista": Finding and Applying VPI Dimensions in the Story

In this part of Chapter Four, we provide you with a guided tour to reflect potential learning about the category "Space and Time" and its corresponding four dimensions (Geographic Advantage, Work Schedule Overlap, Time in Shared Dialogue, and Time Investment), based on elements of our story.

Geographic Advantage

Many geographically dispersed groups face the challenge of time-zone differences. Due to their geographic spread across numerous points between Japan and the Americas, the Beltronik group is one of them. Paolo Azevedo mentions this when he starts his conversation with Patricia Kennedy.

"Well, haven't you noticed we are sort of cut off from the rest of the team?"

"What do you mean?"

"Well, Munich has it really easy. They sit right in the middle of the map and can communicate with the rest of the world over lunch. But we are at the edges and I think they keep on forgetting us."

Consider for a moment: How could one establish a feeling of equality or justice among group members in different locations? Why is that a key ingredient for high virtual performance?

Paolo Azevedo hints at a potential solution when he says, *"Well, first of all, Florian always invites to Munich time. I think it would be considerate to mention our time zones in the invitation as well."*

"Point taken."

"And they usually schedule our meetings in a way that the Asians can still attend at reasonable hours – you know that the Japanese often work until eight at night – while we need to get up at unholy hours. My wife already hates me for it."

Can you think of other possible solutions? How can one ensure group members are not only NOT forgotten but that their time-zone location is perceived as a Geographic Advantage? What do we know about why Patricia Kennedy has relocated and how that is an advantage for the group, even though Atlanta is not necessarily a hub for the company and she is not close to key customers?

Work Schedule Overlap

Directly connected to geographical distances and time-zone differences is the question of how to create overlapping work schedules to enable all members of a dispersed group to work synchronously.

Please consider the following: How can different time zones be turned into an advantage for organizing work in geographically dispersed groups? How can groups integrate this into their set-up right from the beginning? How do these potential measures directly influence other dimensions, for example Geographic Advantage or Shared Leadership?

Paolo Azevedo mentions one potential aspect. *"Pois, when we were all supposed to work together on the first presentation to the board, we moved in the wrong direction."*

"Meaning?"

"Ever heard of follow-the-sun?"

"You're right, come to think of it. We were pressed for time and did not really manage a relay, since we started in Munich and not here."

"Isso!"

"And we didn't really get to include our inputs because Florian still wanted his assistant to go over it before it was show time for the board."

Time Investment

Beyond the potential overlap of work schedules, it is of crucial importance that the time and energy members invest in virtual group work matches the tasks they have to perform. Members' time budgets and their performance will determine that match.

Paolo Azevedo and Patricia Kennedy push hard for this match, trying to use every minute to communicate:

"Before entering the bike store, [Paolo] redials Patricia Kennedy's number for the third time that evening... While traffic on Highway 285 North is becoming heavier, she calls Paolo back."

Another important aspect is the even or fair distribution of work among those group members who invest similar time budgets into the group work. This will depend on the necessary level of transparency with respect to the different time budgets that the group members can invest.

This is something that Paolo Azevedo mentions to Patricia Kennedy, too:

"I felt cheated. And I feel left out now. My work is not recognized as much as it deserves. Should Florian one day be asked to evaluate my performance, he has no clue. And I think others invest far less than I do. From Yuan, for example, we get almost nothing."

What might be potential solutions for this challenge, especially since the energy and Time Investment also needs to be visible and in many cases accounted for or evaluated by the "home" organization?

Time Shared in Dialogue

Last but not least, group development (solving conflicts, making decisions, etc.), as well as the visibility of a group in an organization, requires communication. There can be a wide range of perspectives about how much time members need to spend in synchronous dialogue for them to feel good about the collaboration. A telling example is the futile voice message Paolo Azevedo's leaves on Patricia Kennedy's voicemail after unsuccessfully trying to reach her several times.

Patricia Kennedy is aware of the necessity to switch from asynchronous communication to synchronous dialogue in certain situations when she calls Paolo, especially when it comes to preventing conflict from growing.

"You called several times and I am aware that I still owe you a couple of mails, so I figured it's time for me to act as a responsible member of the Global Virtual Quality Circle."

Consider for a moment: How would you as a leader try to facilitate and reconcile the different needs with respect to using the precious time for synchronous communication within the group? What could one do as a member of a virtual group in order to practice "voicing" and/ or Shared Leadership if these needs are not addressed?

Paolo Azevedo, in turn, is clear on what the Time Shared in Dialogue could be used for.

"How to discuss improving virtual collaboration... ?"

After having analyzed the facets of the four dimensions for virtual performance improvement in the category "Time and Space" in at least one example, we invite you to continue screening the story for further clues on the dimensions of Geographic Advantage, Work Schedule Overlap, Time in Shared Dialogue, and Time Investment.

Having collected more "data", imagine being the leader of this team or an external consultant and ask yourself the following questions:

What would you like to improve and why?

What measures could be used to improve the virtual performance of this group?

How would you bring the topic(s) into the group?

How would you work on it/them?

How would you monitor it/them?

How would you keep the topic(s) alive?

Your Notes

4.8 Coaching Questions for Space and Time

Start with the following questions:

- What is your understanding of the category "Space and Time"? (If needed, it would be good to give some input on "Space and Time".)
- How would you describe the present situation in the group?
- Please describe where the members are located.
- Please describe the different functions and backgrounds of the members.
- Please describe how the members are connected to the rest of the organization.
- How do you think that the members would describe the situation?
- What are your "hopes/wishes/plans" for the group in the future?

Geographic Advantage

- How many members are based in the different locations?
- Where are your internal customers based?
- Where are your external customers based?
- Do you think the balance is good?
- If you could change something regarding the distribution, what would that be?

Work Schedule Overlap

- How is the Work Schedule Overlap in the group at the moment?
- Has the group discussed the overlap?
- Is there a pattern in the group?
- If you could change the Work Schedule Overlap, what would it then look like?
- What would be needed (from your side) to change the existing situation?
- Who do you need to include in the different locations to make changes happen?

Time Shared in Dialog

- How often do you communicate/work together synchronously?
- Which tool(s) do you use to connect?
- Please describe what happens when you work synchronously together?
- Is there a kind of rhythm or "heartbeat" in the group?
- Does everybody in the group have access to the same tools?

Time Investment

- Please go through the following for each group member:
  - How much time (as a percentage) does the member dedicate to this group/topic?
  - Is this enough time?
  - Do you need to change the percentage(s) of time invested?
  - Would it be possible to change the invested time of one or more members?

Notes

1 Maznevski and Chudoba (2000).
2 Cummings and Haas (2012) argue that, in order to be a real team member, one must invest 40 per cent of one's time into the team's work.
3 Maznevski and Chudoba (2000).

Members, Tasks, and Objectives

5.1 The Story: 4th Ring Road

5.2 The Four Dimensions of Members, Tasks, and Objectives

5.3 Language Skills

5.4 Quality of Relationships

5.5 Information Sharing

5.6 Identification with Group and Objectives

5.7 Self Reflection: Lessons Learned from Chapter Five

5.8 Coaching Questions for Members, Tasks, and Objectives

5.1 The Story: 4th Ring Road

Lin will be thrilled. During their next date, he will show her the new catalogue and confess that he has already chosen some of the furniture at Ikea on 4th Ring Road. Next Saturday, they can test the beds there together and then make a decision. And since they can only move into their small apartment on Jingzhu Expressway in four weeks, any delivery bottlenecks won't be a problem.

His Swedish colleague Britt told him that Ikea's business model includes customers' self-assembly of furniture. But many Chinese don't understand the purpose of this. He, too, prefers having his furniture delivered and assembled. Lin and he have better things to do during the weekend than to tighten screws. After all, at 32 he is an adult and just got married.

Hui Yuan has to force himself to forget Lin and 4th Ring Road for a moment, even when this takes an almost inhuman effort. Another "virtual team meeting", as they call it, of the Global Virtual Quality Circle will start in 15 minutes. The team leader, Bell, wants to speak to him on the phone beforehand.

While he has somehow come to like these people, he doesn't feel at ease with the project. His manager, Feng Zhao, had been given the project by his supervisor, Guan, and had only informed him, Hui Yuan, shortly before the first meeting. However, Munich had apparently been informed about his membership weeks before. How embarrassing that he was late for that phone conference and that he couldn't make any substantial contribution.

His situation hasn't really improved since then. Feng Zhao deems the project unimportant for Beijing and doesn't give him the time budget that is necessary to work on the action items agreed upon by the team. Moreover, he has no experience at all with those Internet things except for Sina Weibo (the Chinese Twitter) and Renren (the Chinese Facebook), where Lin and he met and where they posted their wedding photos from last month. And since he can't really contribute, the others will probably become suspicious of him and his role.

There is an upside to the whole thing, though. Thanks to his good work in the evening classes, his English is quite decent compared to the Japanese guy. If only they sent him the meeting topics in advance and spoke more slowly. With whom could he talk about this?

Bell's voice interrupts his thoughts.

"Good evening Hui, how are you? Has the smog eased in Beijing?"

"Ah, smog is not bad right now."

"Hui, I have wanted to ask you: would you prefer me to call you Hui or rather Yuan?"

"Hui is fine, thank you."

"Great, please also call me Florian, then".

"Yes, thank you."

"Hui, before the team gets online I want to briefly discuss language issues with you. Britt and Ranjit have made me aware that we have a lot of room for improvement here. We often act like the whole world speaks English while, in fact, over a billion speak Mandarin."

"Yes?"

"While I am afraid that we will not all be able to learn Mandarin for the scope of this project, nor Japanese for that matter, I would like to discuss with you how we can cater more towards your language needs."

"Yes, that would be most welcome."

"Do you want to do it now or at a later point?"

"Later is good, thank you."

"As you wish! Well, let's go online then and say hello to the team. And you tell them a bit about the great weather you're having in Beijing and also share your thoughts about specific Chinese perspectives on Online Identity, will you?"

5.2 The Four Dimensions of Members, Tasks, and Objectives

This category offers dimensions with a project-management and social-capital focus essential for high degrees of virtual performance.

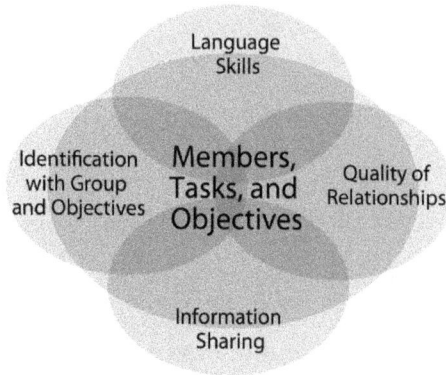

Good project and relationship management is a challenge for any team. While we won't go into much detail about project management, we would like to emphasize that it is essential for virtual groups to have early-warning systems in place, ensure fast reaction times, and have all necessary information when it is needed. Thus *Information Sharing* proactively builds Virtual Closeness and increases performance.

A basic prerequisite for participation in this organizational Information Sharing is quite often overlooked or at least underestimated. It is the level of *Language Skills* that is needed to make sense of information and to be able to articulate oneself.

Furthermore, a person who works simultaneously in local and global projects often faces the experience of multiple others – I and them. What's more, global projects are often not aligned with a person's local workload. The tasks they involve can even be in clear conflict with one's local responsibilities. In order to balance the tension between local and global belonging, *Identification with the Group and its Objectives* is therefore crucial for setting the right priorities.

In the next step, when a group assembles to work from remote locations, its initial experience of collaborating and the trajectory of its development depend to a large extent on the *Quality of the Relationships* between its members. The experiences feeding into this quality strongly influence a group's social capital, including its ability to agree on common goals – an important prerequisite of member identification with the group and its objectives.

5.3 Language Skills

As anyone who has worked in a virtual group can confirm, the quality of the exchange permitted by the working language shared by group members is absolutely central to good collaboration. Even in monolingual groups, experts from different topical areas may literally speak different technical languages. Thus Language Skills also encompass the shared understanding of relevant technical terms. The standard language in global virtuality, however, is English, and skill levels and variety in usage often differ dramatically.

On the other hand, having a multilingual group is also of great benefit to global communication, and the potential inherent in that ought to be tapped by organizations. In this chapter, we will show how we operationalize these ideas.

Textbox 5.1: Definition: Dimension "Language Skills"

The degree to which members are able to adjust their language skills to the level of other members and work-related challenges.

Item 1: The degree to which members are used to working in international settings where different language skills are present.

This item addresses questions like: How familiar are members with the fact that other members have different levels of the shared language and different accents? Do members feel comfortable asking for clarification if things are difficult to understand? Are members comfortable with the fact that they are not native speakers?

Item 2: The degree to which members successfully adjust their language skills to the level of other members and work-related challenges.

This item addresses questions like: Are members capable of adjusting the language used to the level of the other members? Do members use simpler words when talking to other members to ensure the message comes across? Do members use additional means to ensure their message comes across (such as handouts, visualization and paraphrasing)?

Good Practice

In an intercultural group, effectively exchanging information crucially depends on the level of Language Skills of individual members and how different language levels are taken into account. Language is a basic condition for participating in a global group. While working with interpreters/translators is always an option, it does not provide for a sustainable long-term way of working together.

The challenge for global groups is to reach a level of language proficiency (usually in English) that allows for effective performance while keeping expectations realistic. The goal is not to get everyone to speak like a native but to create a setting in which different accents, dialects, and skill levels support smooth performance rather than hinder it.

To see how this can be operationalized, consider our youth. Youth across the globe communicate virtually, and often this is done in English. Grammar and spelling become subordinate to the chief goal of exchanging information, which is reached with a limited set of basic vocabulary. While this is sometimes taken to the extreme, adding fuel to the fire of the discourse on linguistic impoverishment, the basic principle is very effective. When we concentrate on exchanging information and allow ourselves to let go of native speakers' standards of linguistic refinement, we can get the actual work done. Successful virtual collaboration is about communicative competence and not about linguistic competence. Because of that, native speakers can in fact cause more friction in communication processes than non-natives. And pacing native speakers is a real challenge.

A simple strategy is to use as few words as possible when explaining important matters, relying on icons, symbols, pictures, schemes, graphics, and videos that have the same meaning in different languages.

Implementing multiple feedback loops to check whether the message came across as intended is also very useful. These could include the following questions:

Having heard our suggestion:

- What would be the first things you could do?

- How would you paraphrase what was said in your own words?

Our Advice

The following steps will help to diminish language problems:

✓ Provide different parallel communication channels. In addition to a phone or video conference, always ensure that a real-time, text-based channel (a chat, instant-messaging or application sharing channel) for asking questions and sharing opinions is provided. This is particularly helpful for members who, for language or cultural reasons, want to put their contributions in writing to articulate themselves.

✓ Ask the native speakers to write the minutes during the meeting and make them visible to all participants. This will slow down the speed of their speech and give non-native speakers the chance to understand better what's being said and written.

✓ Create a virtual team handbook on the intranet to document the most important terminology and abbreviations used.

✓ In virtual meetings as well as in documents and other presentations, visualize as much as possible in order to decrease verbal language and increase mutual understanding. Use graphic facilitation methods on flip charts or smart boards.

✓ Record online conversations and convert them into podcasts for later listening.

✓ Build a culture in which it's ok to interrupt someone and ask them to repeat or explain what they are saying.

✓ Provide group members with the time and other resources to learn the standard language of their global group.

✓ Allow for breakout sessions in homogenous language groups to enable all participants to confirm their understanding of what has been said.

Textbox 5.2: Do You Speak Globish?

Having mastered a language, whether it is our native or a foreign one, we tend to speak it on a high level using refined vocabulary and grammar, and often "slang". A non-native speaker whose English skills are proficient or just basic may have difficulties understanding more complex English in an international business context. A lack of English-language skills can strongly impede global virtual teamwork. Therefore, we strongly recommend using "Globish" – *Glob*al Engl*ish*, as developed by Jean-Paul Nerriere and David Hon. As they state on their website, www.globish. com, "The simple goal of Globish is to reach only a level – a common ground – where everyone understands everyone else, everywhere in the world."

Globish makes do with only 1,500 words, meaning that more sophisticated vocabulary is substituted by simpler, paraphrasing words. The basic rules include:

Keep sentences short	Avoid negative questions
Repeat yourself	Avoid all humour
Avoid metaphors and colourful expressions	
Avoid acronyms	Use gestures and visual aids

(http://www.globish.com/?page=about_globish&lang=en_utf8)

While Globish might facilitate a better understanding and thus more meaningful processes in a group, it often comes at the price of losing humour or colourful language. Humour is important for good communication and can be slowly developed as group members get to know each other better.

> ➢ Once we were providing online support to a global SAP implementation team. The British colleagues used to joke a lot and spoke in slang. When addressing this fact, it turned out that the jokes and phrases came from the realm of cricket, the British national sport. In order to include the non-British members, we created an informal communication space where the British colleagues explained cricket and created a cricket glossary. Some of the cricket lingo has since become common group insider language and members now better understand the jokes – a great step towards building a Purple Space.

5.4 Quality of Relationships

Needless to say, the Quality of Relationships within a virtual group is essential for high performance. In some cultures, having established functioning relationships is a precondition even for engaging in collaboration. A relationship is similar to a bank account. When a person deposits sufficient funds, she can take them out when she needs them, for example when she is looking for a contact. If she has a good experience, she is likely to open new accounts.

This metaphor brings to attention one team-development phase that is often overlooked: the ending phase. While this phase is only relevant when a group stops working together and members move to other working places, thinking ahead towards the ending is an important competence of the virtual leader. In the ending phase, the group should review the quality of the shared process and the corresponding results. Learning for the future and being able to close open ends in their relationships through review and reflection lay the basis for consolidating the social capital that was built during the collaboration. Rather than starting from scratch, this allows former group members who come together in a new context to build on their existing relationships. This can speed up the new group's development process towards high performance. This section deals with these aspects.

Good Practice

In order to unlock the potential of a group's social capital it must be valued, sometimes even assessed using mapping tools, and relationships need to be managed. If people are in unresolved conflict or just don't feel at ease with others in their group, then that needs to be voiced and discussed without blaming or risking loss of face or honour. This strongly links back to inclusion and the ability to respect diverse work and Communication Styles.

Especially in long-term cooperation, relationship building must be a priority from day one. Having an appreciative exchange about group members' experiences of previous international collaborative settings as well as working relationships will help them to cope with past and future challenges. Capitalizing on the positive experiences will pave the road towards high performance. Facilitated collection and reflection of those experiences – through the method of Appreciative Inquiry, for example – will create a solid base for further improving the Quality of Relationships. Regular review sessions will help to assess and continuously develop the quality of cooperating.

As for the widespread practice of building relationships between virtual group members face-to-face, increasing numbers of organizations now start with relationship-building measures *before* group members meet face-to-face for the first time. We strongly recommend conducting the kick off for a virtual group online. Contrary to popular belief, this promises better performance than a face-to-face kick off. A virtual kick off signals that virtuality is the reality wherein a group will work. Precious face-to-face time is better saved for making important decisions and solving conflict.

> ➤ A global automotive supplier conducts web conferences to kick off virtual group work. Group members fill in an "All about me" card, including a secret they would like to share about themselves. The card is presented to colleagues during the web conference.

Our Advice

In the following, we concentrate on some of those aspects of relationship building that are unique to global cooperation scenarios.

Particularly in network organizations, it is useful for group members to understand which networks their colleagues belong to and what they mean to them. This places individuals in their social context. In addition to those social links, a network diagram will show who has worked with whom before and visualize the existing ties within a group. Such a relationship map can also be used as a diagnostic tool to depict Virtual Closeness in metric terms in order to define the distance between network members. In that context, relationship management means identifying the mission-critical ties of members, the degree of closeness between them, and whether this should be improved. This approach is often used in coaching situations.

In addition to building relationships through the formal channels of project work, members should be given adequate Space and Time to get to know each other informally. This requires the clear delineation of formal and informal communication spaces.

> ➤ The HR department of one of our clients, a global producer of technology, has introduced a talent network and a corresponding

platform on the intranet, hoping that this would forge an organization-wide community of potential future leaders. The challenge in bringing such communities to life lays in attracting active members. While there are corporate interests behind the community, the talents also have individual needs to communicate with each other. Being a member of a formal talent community is a one-dimensional reason that might not create enough motivation to join. An additional informal element is needed to create interest, for example through connecting with each other on LinkedIn or other social-media platforms. That way, members can build relationships that are potentially valuable throughout their careers. A network's attractiveness is further increased when top management is present in both the formal and informal forums. This enhances members' visibility and the community's relevance to the organization's objectives.

A look at the younger generations helps to understand how virtual relationships are built and maintained rapidly and effortlessly. They meet in informal spaces and play together online. One important defining aspect is that they have no reservations about virtual communication and thus no resistance to it. In that way, they are role models for Virtual Closeness.

> The younger colleagues in one of our client's organizations play online "Bullshit Bingo" during meetings. The point is to catch typical behaviours of organizational members or business-lingo phrases that are often perceived as empty (such as "high performance", "cost saving", and "best practice") or behaviours like calling in from one's car. The first to have three such behaviours or phrases on the Bingo sheet wins. This is an example of a fun game that has two functions: playing together online increases Virtual Closeness. And it can increase concentration on the task on hand.

> When building three-dimensional virtual spaces for a major automotive company for training (role plays) and cooperation (group rooms) purposes, we also implemented informal spaces. In addition to official group spaces and lecture halls where people work and learn, we also included a beach with a bar where people could hang out between learning sessions.

Relationship management is a central leadership task and done most successfully when it takes a strengths-based approach[1] and focuses on authenticity. However, working and communicating in the virtual world raises a vital question: how do people manage the impact of moving into the virtual realm on their professional identity? Effective virtual collaboration requires leaders who are successfully managing relationships in both worlds – a quality that doesn't always come easily. Having a positive leadership identity in the face-to-face world doesn't automatically imply the same in virtuality. There are people who are rarely noticed in face-to-face meetings but are great e-moderators of virtual spaces – "speaking with their fingers on the keyboard" – and vice versa.

5.5 Information Sharing

Against the background of a group's heartbeat, the exchange of information is a group's bloodstream that provides every part of the organism with the necessary data and energy for the fulfilment of its function. Information exchange is a two-sided coin concerning the responsibilities around it: information push and information pull. This difference also determines the media to be used. Information-push media include email and newsletters; information-pull media include WIKIs and shared data spaces.

Textbox 5.4: Definition: Dimension "Information Sharing"

This dimension describes the degree to which members have access to work-relevant information and share it proactively.

Item 1: The degree to which important work information is available to all members who need it.

This item addresses questions like: Are data rooms accessible for members according to their needs? Do group members know where to find relevant information? Do members provide data in a way others can interpret and use?

Item 2: The degree to which members share all work-relevant information proactively.

This item addresses questions like: Do members proactively share relevant information with the rest of the group's members? Is all information accessible to every member or is some of the information only for part of the group? Do members know which information is important to whom within the group? Are some members concerned that information within the group could be misused?

How an organization thinks and shares information is often symbolized through the general, underlying dichotomy "Us and Them". In many organizations, this cognitive and emotional separation between individuals and groups leads to a culture in which information is used as a power instrument: the power is with those who have it and they exercise their power by deciding how much information to share and with whom. On the other hand, not everyone benefits from getting every single piece of information. Just think of the information overload that often results from pervasive ccing of emails. To balance this tension, especially in virtual collaboration where the perception of lacking transparency and being excluded can develop quickly, it is imperative that organizations and groups build a culture that transcends the dichotomy "Us and Them".

> ➢ One of our clients is a global energy provider. When a new leader took over one of the country offices, the local staff was upset when it realized that it was not the first to be informed about the leadership change. This made clear that within their organization, country offices thought of each other as "Us and Them".

> ➢ Another client group that is part of a global online market player was struggling with the basic duality that exists in most organizational settings: "Us and Them". The two sub-groups are located in the US and the UK. While they cooperated, they didn't really communicate and collaborate. The ensuing feeling of being disconnected made Virtual Closeness very difficult to build. We therefore focused on introducing and practising how to develop a culture of regular, fearless, and respectful *voicing* of concerns, criticism, recognition, etc. (see Chapter Two).

Once people are aligned and working towards the same goal, they are more likely to *share information* of relevance and necessity with all members – another inevitable function of managing a project well and a great step towards Shared Leadership.

Good Practice

Effective collaboration strongly depends on people's readiness and ability to share information relevant to their work with other group members. This presupposes a number of beneficial circumstances, including the following.

In order to proactively share relevant information with others, it is important to have knowledge of their context and informational demands. Hence group members should have a good understanding not only of their own but also of their colleagues' tasks – also a necessary basis for implementing Shared Leadership.

Information Sharing works best when all relevant information is stored in one central spot and is available to all stakeholders. An excellent index or search engine where documents can be found easily is another option. This also implies that members are able to provide information and knowledge in a way that can be understood by others without further explanation.

> ➢ Customers sometimes ask us to share our expertise on how to create learning material for self-organized, web-based learning to enable knowledge managers or groups to build their own knowledge repository. A good method is the *webquest* movement created by teachers that is based on the theory of minimal informational texts and the guiding questions around them.

While group members are urged to share information and its location proactively, information flooding (for example, through superfluous ccing) must be avoided.

Our Advice

Clarity is especially required about two aspects. First, it is important for groups to know the information profiles of all their members: who needs which information for what work. Second, group members need to know how the pushing and/or pulling of information is distributed and regulated in their group. Is information proactively shared and obtained or do the local cultures of some group members rely on managers and other group members to ask for it? With this information available, group members should be able to create documents that are self-explanatory to others.

The benefit of having informal in addition to formal communication channels also applies to Information Sharing. Some information is best shared formally, other pieces informally.

> ➤ One of our clients is a European group that is part of a global online retailer. A leader located in the Paris office manages a very successful virtual group spread around the globe that excels at using media to simulate reality. Specifically, he introduced a group-chat function for private, internal exchange. In an office, we can easily approach a colleague next door to discuss ideas and ask for input – a crucial function of creativity. Obviously, this is not so easy in virtual groups. The manager therefore implemented chat rooms wherein group members could interact by asking questions and exchanging information, thereby helping each other in real time. What made this model so successful, however, is that this group also uses the chat room for social interaction facilitated by the leader. When arriving at the office on Monday mornings, group members briefly enter the social chat room to greet colleagues and share a bit about their weekend – just what they would do if they were collocated in one office. Moreover, "insider" information is exchanged via the chat, keeping everyone in the loop about what's going on in the different country offices.

The disadvantage of sharing too much information that is not of use or interest to everyone is best described in the following example.

> ➤ Another client group had regular Friday meetings dreaded by most members. Those meetings took four hours, during which every participant reported for half an hour on developments in their respective locations, including information about customers, key accounts, etc. Nobody really listened to what was being said because most of the information, apart from being presented in an unattractive way, was not deemed relevant by others. Having regular meetings for the sole purpose of sharing information is

not useful. Pure information is best shared in writing; listening to it is not necessary. In (virtual) meetings, many people are attentive during the first five to ten minutes. If they have no chance to become involved until then, most start focusing on other matters like answering their emails.

The solution for this group rested on a profound change in the meeting setup. Meeting time was reduced to two hours; the initial information exchange was turned into gossip about the week's events in the different locations; and the actual information had to be sold: everyone who had something to say was asked to write it down in a document that was shared in the common data space. They then had slots of five minutes to sell their information to the others, arguing why this information is important and should be read. Opinions were exchanged the following week. Suddenly, it became interesting to participate in the Friday meetings, mainly because insider information normally confined to water-cooler and coffee-machine areas was shared and an informal atmosphere appropriate for a Friday was created.

Assembling group members around virtual fireplaces is another way of improving the process of Information Sharing. More and more companies actively pursue a strategy for keeping group-relevant information in one place with the help of social media or dedicated group ware.

In many cultures, information is only considered relevant when it is not written. In countries such as Spain or Brazil it is therefore essential to keep informal information channels open at all times.

5.6 Identification with Group and Objectives

This dimension is derived from classical team development and project management and cannot be neglected in virtual settings. It is also found in Jessica Lipnack and Jeffrey Stamps'[2] work that identified the success factors of virtual teams as aligning *people* and *purpose*. They added a third notion, that of *links*, to adapt the model to the specific characteristics of the virtual world. Here, we suggest substituting the notion of links with our concept of Purple Space.

Textbox 5.5: Definition: Dimension "Identification with Group and Objectives"

This dimension describes the degree to which members identify with the group and its objectives.

Item 1: The degree to which members feel part of and identify themselves with the group.

This item addresses questions like: Are members proud to be part of this group? Would they tend to prioritize the issues of this group ahead of those of other groups? Do members use symbols or communication styles unique to this group?

Item 2: The degree to which members identify themselves with the work-related objectives of the group.

This item addresses questions like: Do members know the purpose of the collaboration within the group? Are members able to explain the group's objectives to others? Are members motivated by their objectives to perform outstandingly in the context of the group? Do members know and value their own contribution and those of the other members?

Good Practice

Reaching high performance is also dependent on group members' identification with their group and the group's goals. Identification happens when being part of a group is perceived as attractive, for example because of learning opportunities, career opportunities, or other reasons. Identification results in a sense of shared responsibility for the planned outcomes and the other group members.

Having leadership support to align global and local demands is therefore indispensable and requires that local managers of global group members come on board, too. If they understand what their group members are doing on a global level and why, they will hopefully provide the necessary structural support. This is particularly important in matrix and network organizations that feed on vital tensions between numerous connections and cooperation levels. These tensions make it difficult to identify with the group and its objectives. Clarifying objectives and guidelines for the group and its projected outcomes must therefore be a high priority throughout the cooperation.

In an intercultural context, it is not always easy to achieve a shared understanding of the group's goals and objectives, even when using the same words. Very different mental models might define individual and group culture and language. In a sentence like, "The prototype will be ready on January 3rd", the meaning of "prototype" might significantly differ depending on whether a German or Latin American engineer uses it. The same is true about the understanding of what constitutes a deadline: "Do we have an extra week or day beyond January 3rd?"

Our Advice

Creating a shared understanding of goals and objectives requires exploring the cultural concepts that determine individual understanding and action. In the above example, this can mean asking each member to explain her or his understanding of "prototype" and "deadline", what constitutes an agreeable deviation from a deadline, and how to deal with delays.

Another important and often overlooked aspect is the importance of learning how to work in virtuality from the very start of a virtual collaborative project. Virtuality will be the everyday reality of a global, virtual group and they need to start in that very environment. Agreeing on objectives, planning the project, negotiating work schedule and media – all this could and should be done virtually. If a virtual group starts with a face-to-face meeting to plan all of this, there will always be an experience of deficit once the virtual work begins. The first face-to-face meeting should therefore take place a few months *after* a virtual group has started working together.

> ➤ One of our clients has created a standardized support process including online facilitation for the forming, storming, and norming phases of its virtual groups. This process is entirely based on web conferences and individual web-based learning of intercultural communication and virtual cooperation.

Identification with the Purple Space wherein a virtual group meets to work doesn't stop during break times.

> ➤ One of our client groups uses the Wii play station to link up during break times. That way, they connect during their breaks, just as collocated groups do, and they even exercise, which benefits their health and positively impacts performance.

Some remarks on the concept of Purple Space in the context of the dimension Identification with Group and Objectives

The very existence of a Purple Space is a sign for members' identification with their group and its objectives, which, in turn, takes place in the Purple Space. Cooperation usually passes through three stages on the way to a mature Purple Space. Every stage is characterized by the extent of identification:

1. You work on your own.

2. You accept – or choose – local cooperation.

3. You realize the necessity of global cooperation.

Part of this realization is the acknowledgment that deconstructing local success may be indispensable for achieving global success. This is what makes global cooperation so difficult. Consider the earlier example of an organization that decides to centralize all human resources policies and functions on a global level. Local HR departments may find this change very difficult to embrace because they will be asked to give up a well-functioning HR practice in order to adapt global policies. To them, this may mean letting go of a local success model in favour of creating global one.

This goes hand in hand with the formation of a global Purple Space where global thinking prevails and which provides the technical means (the "links") to realize global cooperation.

Within this newly created global collaboration space, defining a purpose for cooperating is equally important. While the official purpose will be defined by the project's objectives, people will often commit themselves to filling the Purple Space with life only when they define a personal purpose that connects them with their colleagues. This can be something to fix or fight against (the "common enemy"), or it can be a career opportunity, learning to use new media, or just the social capital within the group.

Global cooperation is key to changing an organizational culture. Developing from individual or local cooperation to global cooperation is difficult, if not impossible, in the climate of friendly avoidance or mistrust which often characterizes organizational changes. When management fails to explain the reasons underlying globalization processes, change may lead to increased mistrust and can quickly run into enormous resistance. Therefore, developing a Purple Space is about voicing, including diversity, and creating Virtual Closeness – prerequisites leading to trustworthy relations among group members.

The concept of Purple Space with its corresponding dynamics is meaningfully linked to the concept of change management. Successful change management in processes of organizational globalization rests on working with all members to create understanding and support for the change. The first step is creating the Purple Space wherein this change process can successfully evolve. Building this framework is a central leadership task.

Moreover, corporate values play a crucial role in global cooperation. If an organization manages to establish universal corporate values that define its work internationally and are supported by all members across the globe, these values can function as a steering tool in the Purple Spaces. They become part of Purple Spaces and define them, filling them with basic signposts that guide the building of a new culture of collaborating.

5.7 Self Reflection: Lessons Learned from Chapter Five: "4th Ring Road": Finding and Applying VPI Dimensions in the Story

In this part of Chapter Five, we provide you with a guided tour to reflect potential learning about the category "Members, Tasks, and Objectives" and its corresponding four dimensions (Language Skills, Quality of Relationships, Information Sharing, and Identification with Group and Objectives), based on elements of our story.

Language Skills

As profane as it may sound, Language Skills are an integral challenge for many virtual teams, groups, and networks operating internationally. This issue also lurks beneath the communication surface of the Beltronik group in our story.

Even though we learn that Hui Yuan considers addressing his own language challenges and those of his Japanese colleague (*With whom could he talk about this... ?*), he doesn't react when Florian Bell directly addresses it. *"Hui, before the team gets online I want to briefly discuss language issues with you. Britt and Ranjit have made me aware that we have a lot of room for improvement here. We often act like the whole world speaks English while, in fact, over a billion speak Mandarin."*

"Yes?"

"While I am afraid that we will not all be able to learn Mandarin for the scope of this project, nor Japanese for that matter, I would like to discuss with you how we can better cater to your language needs."

"Yes, that would be most welcome."

"Do you want to do it now or at a later point?"

"Later is good, thank you."

> What could be potential reasons for Hui Yuan not wanting to discuss the matter over the phone at this point in time? Please consider the following: there is more to communication than what is verbally expressed and received. What advice can we give Florian Bell on how to deal with this situation in the future? How could these challenges be addressed in the set-up and/or facilitation of an international group?

Information Sharing

Directly linked to Language Skills is the dimension of Information Sharing. One aspect of this is that we cannot share information if we don't feel comfortable with the media used or the degree of Language Skills required for this.

Hui Yuan is our prototype for this kind of challenge. *Moreover, he has no experience at all with those Internet things except for Sina Weibo (the Chinese Twitter) and Renren (the Chinese Facebook), where Lin and he met and where they posted their wedding photos from last month.*

More important, however, is the fact that we can only proactively share information if we know what kind of information others currently need. This, in turn, requires that the group members have a sound overview of running processes and their corresponding statuses.

This becomes apparent when Hui Yuan reflects his situation. *There is an upside to the whole thing, though. Thanks to his good work in the evening classes his English is quite decent compared to the Japanese guy. If only they sent him the meeting topics in advance and spoke more slowly. With whom could he talk about this?*

Please go back to our story. Hui Yuan knows what would help him to share information and also ask for information more quickly, but does not express it. What is it? How could you as a member of a virtual group ensure that Information Sharing is facilitated? How is Information Sharing directly linked to Virtual Closeness?

Quality of Relationships

The degree to which we share information and contribute to the group work and the degree to which we perceive our relationships as meaningful and attractive are directly linked.

Hui Yuan intuitively feels this connection. *And since he can't really contribute, the others will probably become suspicious of him and his role.*

Hui Yuan's heart and thoughts are obviously more occupied by his new wife, Lin, and his new living situation than by the group and its members, tasks, and objectives.

While this is understandable, what reasons (apart from his personal priorities) might explain why *he has somehow come to like these people [but] doesn't feel at ease with the project?*

Hui Yuan's thoughts reveal that he may not be a good match for the task, which makes it hard for him to feel that he can really add value as a member. *Moreover, he has no experience at all with those Internet things except for Sina Weibo (the Chinese Twitter) and Renren (the Chinese Facebook), where Lin and he met and where they posted their wedding photos from last month. And since he can't really contribute, the others will probably become suspicious of him and his role.*

Quality of Relationships has two central aspects. The social capital that members have accumulated in former work experiences with international partners and the quality of interactions of members on topics that are not work-related. Hui Yuan is bound to score low on both because he has been with the company for just one year and has had few opportunities or time to engage in work-unrelated interactions with other group members.

> Considering that we cannot turn back the clock and exclude Yuan from the project without major face-loss of many involved stakeholders, how could we strengthen the first aspect of Quality of Relationships at least to a small degree and the second aspect to a larger degree? How does Florian Bell try to improve the quality of his relationship with Yuan and why does he seem to fail? What could he do, perhaps with the help of others members, to make the project and the group more attractive for Yuan from a relationship angle?

Identification with Group and Objectives

Hui Yuan has mixed feelings when it comes to identifying with the group and its objectives: *he has somehow come to like these people [but] doesn't feel at ease with the project.*

He somehow identifies with the group but hasn't had enough time yet to get a feeling for the project framework. He doubts whether he can add value to the group and that is a very important prerequisite for identifying with the project.

His manager, Feng Zhao, had been given the project by his supervisor, Guan, and had only informed him, Hui Yuan, shortly before the first meeting. However, Munich had apparently been informed about his membership weeks before. How embarrassing that he was late for that phone conference and that he couldn't make any substantial contribution.

Further, while the Quality of Relationships can also be influenced on interpersonal levels, the alignment of objectives and potentially conflicting roles and identities often cause challenges in a larger organizational frame. The underlying organizational dynamics make it even more difficult for Yuan to identify with the group's objectives and the corresponding work packages. *His situation hasn't really improved since then. Feng Zhao deems the project unimportant for Beijing and doesn't give him the time budget that is necessary to work on the action items agreed upon by the team.*

How could Florian Bell improve Hui Yuan's identification with the group and its objectives, given that he is already part of the group? What could group leaders generally do during the start-up phase of a group (e.g. team kick off), during the collaboration, and at the end of a group process to ensure a strong degree of identification? How could the development of a Purple Space accelerate and deepen identification?

After analyzing the facets of the four dimensions for virtual performance improvement in the category "Members, Tasks, and Objectives" in at least one example, we invite you to continue screening the story for further clues on the dimensions of Language Skills, Quality of Relationships, Information Sharing, and Identification with Group and Objectives.

Having collected more "data", imagine being the leader of this team or an external consultant and ask yourself the following questions:

What would you like to improve and why?
What could be a measure for the improvement of the virtual performance of this group?
How would you bring the topic(s) into the group?
How would you work on it/them?
How would you monitor it/them?
How would you keep the topic(s) alive?

Your Notes

5.8 Coaching Questions for Members, Tasks, and Objectives

Start with the following questions:

- What is your understanding of the category "Members, Tasks, and Objectives"?
  (If needed, it would be good to give some input on "Members, Tasks, and Objectives")
- How would you describe the present situation in the group?
- Could you please describe the objectives and the task of the group?
- Do all members have the same interest in the objectives and tasks?
- If you could choose, what would you like to change in the group?
- How do you think the members would describe the situation?
- What are your "hopes/wishes/plans" for the group in the future?

Quality of Relationships

- Please describe the relationships in the group.
- What would be needed to develop a stronger relationship inside the group?
- How could you proactively support this process?
- How could you involve the group members to take part in this process?

Information Sharing

- Which members have access to which kind of information?
- Which members share which kind of information with each other?
- If there are imbalances, what could be the reason for this?
- How could you support a more balanced approach?
- Who would be needed to change this situation?

Identification with Group and Objectives

- How much do you think that the members identify themselves with the group and its objectives?

- How do you think the members would describe the situation regarding the identification?
- What do you think is needed to increase the identification within the group and with regard to the objectives?
- Are the group's objectives aligned with the local objectives of the members?
- What and who is needed locally to ensure an alignment with the objectives of the individuals and the group?

Language Skills

- How can you support the development of the members' Language Skills?
- How can you overcome an imbalance in Language Skills until the skills are developed?
- What can you actively do to support members to contribute despite different language skill levels?
- How do you employ different media in order to ensure support for different Language Skills?
- How do you employ visualization methods to support different language levels?
- How do you support skills like paraphrasing and active listening to ensure that different language levels do not lead to misunderstandings?

Notes

1 Rath and Conchie (2009).
2 Lipnack and Stamps (2000).

CHAPTER SIX

● ●

E-Culture

6.1   The Story: Is It Honne?

6.2   The Four Dimensions of E-Culture

6.3   Virtual Experiences

6.4   Global Netiquette Skills

6.5   Media Competence

6.6   Online Identity Competence

6.7   Self Reflection: Lessons Learned from Chapter Six

6.8   Coaching Questions for E-Culture

6.1 The Story: Is It Honne?

The young Chinese has sent him another chat message, as he calls it. At least he notices the messages now. Until recently, because he didn't know that his computer has this function, his chat window was always closed. In spite of the tensions between the two great nations created by their past, Kenji Sakamoto is grateful for Hui Yuan's efforts to save the face of the East Asians against the Western dominance in the team.

Two weeks ago, Hui Yuan gave him a one-on-one introduction to the media used in the team. He was embarrassed about his first attempts at using the Internet, but he never really needed it for his production job at Beltronik. His grandchildren are light years ahead of him in this regard and save the family's honour when it comes to using media. Japan is generally advanced at using web-based applications. One of his sons, Roshi, even develops "avatars" – "virtual representations of real-life protagonists", as he calls them – based on popular Manga heroes. Unfortunately, he is in touch with Roshi only seldom since he moved to Richmond, California.

He has noticed that the members of the Global Virtual Quality Circle have been trying even harder to win his favour since the last meeting. It is not quite Kaizen but they are making progress. The feeling that the Westerners as well as Gupta, who is really Americanized, understand each other better still prevails. But this is understandable given that some of them have known each other from previous projects. They are now making an effort to use simple English and send important information in advance so that Yuan, Azevedo, and he can translate it before the meetings.

Another issue is that, in virtuality, he comes across like a ghost. "Honne", one's true voice, is not audible. Only "tatemae", one's façade, makes an appearance.* Some people call this a lack of authenticity. To him it means that being oneself comes less naturally. After twenty years of supervising others, a certain way of being silent or the movement of an eyebrow can send messages to his co-workers and colleagues in a way that words could not. Can he change this? Does he want to change this? Perhaps he ought to talk about this to Gupta, who has a decent age and, unlike himself, moves between the worlds.

Hui Yuan's message is still blinking on the screen. It reads:

"Move into new apt. on Friday. Wife \\^o^/."

He is doing it again! Yuan constantly includes symbols that he doesn't understand. And the longer they know each other, the more symbols he uses. It had started with the symbol (^_^)?

---

* The Japanese words **honne** and **tatemae** describe the contrast between a person's true feelings and desires (*honne*) and the behaviour and opinions one displays in public (*tatemae*, literally "façade").

His grandchildren explained to him that these symbols are called "emoticons". They express feelings in informal texts such as emails or chat. In Japan, the younger generation often uses emoticons. His generation, by contrast, was taught that controlling one's emotions is a sign of strength.

Yuan's question mark, for example, can be understood both as a question mark and as a hand scratching a head to express thoughtfulness. One uses this emoticon when incapable of understanding something or when the other doesn't express himself clearly, thereby avoiding direct criticism.

How should he deal with this in the future? The Brazilian and the American also used symbols that his grandchildren, however, had not seen before.

Yuan has been so obliging, almost like a son; he wants to answer him quickly to avoid disappointing him. Almost automatically, his fingers find the right combination on the keyboard:

"Happy for you! \^o^/"

Whether it's honne finding its way through the ether or not, he doesn't know. But it doesn't feel wrong.

6.2 The Four Dimensions of E-Culture

This category focuses on the dimensions that are necessary for the development of high performance in a group's interactions in the virtual part of the shared collaborative (purple) space.

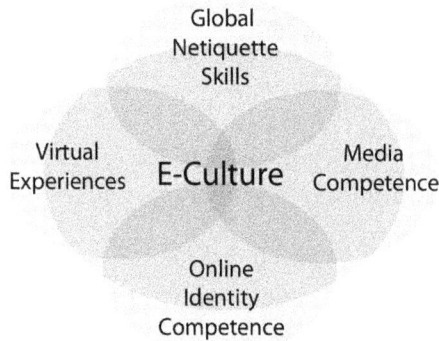

Global
Netiquette
Skills

Virtual
Experiences **E-Culture** Media
Competence

Online
Identity
Competence

E-Culture denotes the basic ability (HOW) to connect virtually. Its quality is influenced by the past *Virtual Experiences* of group members, including their ability to build and manage relationships over distance. Being visible, listened to, and being perceived as human beings in virtuality requires people to create an authentic and professional *Online Identity*.

Based on members' experiences and personal preferences, a set of guidelines for working together across diversity – *Global Netiquette Skills* – needs to be negotiated by the group or set by the leader. And as we saw earlier, establishing a functioning E-Culture demands that all members acquire a high level of *Media Competence*.

> ➤ A group that forms to cooperate virtually can be compared to people settling temporarily in an uninhabited space. Men and women from different regions and cultures decide to inhabit a new "planet" collectively – the Purple Space. To create a peaceful normality, they will need to negotiate a set of guidelines based on past experiences or follow existing global ethical principles (Global Netiquette Skills) to regulate cohabitation and fill the Purple Space. The emerging individual and collective identities will be shaped by

inhabitants' behaviour and their underlying presence in daily life. The new planet also offers unknown resources (new media) that need to be mastered.

6.3 Virtual Experiences

Our attitudes, our professional identity, and especially our openness to new approaches and new media depend on our past experiences of similar contexts. They form a framework that should be taken into account from the beginning of a group process and that informs the setting up of a group's collaborative E-Culture. This dimension therefore addresses the amount and quality of group members' experiences with virtual work. While the younger generations usually have ample online experience, more mature group members may find it difficult to communicate or work in virtuality. The challenge is to explore and acknowledge the range of experiences within a group and ensure that everyone has the skill set needed to perform efficiently.

Textbox 6.1: Definition: Dimension "Virtual Experiences"

The degree to which members have accumulated crucial experience in virtual cooperation and employ the developed skills actively.

Item 1: The degree to which members have had positive experiences of working in online/virtual communication.

This item addresses questions like: Are members aware of their experiences working with virtual communication? If so, what was the context? Did members have experiences with successful virtual communication? Are the members able to specify what the positive aspects and the consequences were?

Item 2: The degree to which members have developed good virtual communication and cooperation practices.

This item addresses questions like: From their previous experiences working with virtual communication, can members deduce factors and behaviours that are critical for successful virtual communication? Are members able to transfer this knowledge into new contexts? Are members able to communicate successfully and cooperate with the group for a longer period (e.g. three months) without any face-to-face contact? Do members sometimes have the impression that parts of the virtual communication are more rewarding or intense than certain face-to-face communication/cooperation processes?

Good Practice

The nature of the experiences we make determine the human psyche and corresponding behaviours. Experiences are stored in the brain and often create unconscious blueprints that lead us to view subsequent experiences through the lens of the previous ones. Hence experiences of, and attitudes towards, virtual collaboration very likely determine a group's individual and collective experience of being virtually connected. Having no experience with working virtually is also an important experience, by the way. Sharing experiences of virtuality – both positive and challenging ones – openly among a group is a good way to create closeness and identify possible behavioural patterns that might be of future importance to the group's productivity.

Our Advice

When a new virtual group is started, previous experiences of working virtually should be exchanged. Similar to reflecting on previous experiences with workplace relationships (see Chapter Five), understanding the technological skill levels of all group members and any possible reservations or fears is crucial for building a Purple Space. This reflection remains crucial for the entire duration of a virtual project. Skills need to be developed continuously, with on-going voicing and feedback.

Training virtual interaction is best done synchronously, enlisting the more experienced group members as coaches or trainers. A virtual group should use overlapping work schedule time to share experiences and identify good practice for working together virtually. They should practise the technology they will use for collaborating in a dedicated and supportive manner. It is particularly important not to use a new medium without practice. Rather, the first meeting with the new medium should be used to identify good practice for applying the new medium. Groups should pick a medium that all members can work with.

Spending time together to share previous experiences and practise virtual work is essential for building the Purple Space. Think of it as setting up a shared office space. This is usually done jointly to ensure that everyone feels comfortable. Establishing the work environment together provides a sound basis for the following dimensions.

6.4 Global Netiquette Skills

When attending a face-to-face meeting, most people observe certain behavioural norms. In most European countries and the US, for example, one knows where to go, arrives five to ten minutes in advance, and greets those present in the room. If people have to travel to meetings they (the people and the meeting) are usually well prepared with an agenda and presentation slides, for example.

In virtuality, these norms often don't exist and people tend to act less considerately. This is especially the case at the beginning of a virtual collaboration when groups and particularly their leaders are often impatient and want things to work immediately. One of the most widespread complaints in this context is about virtual collaboration taking up too much time and being inefficient. However, when thinking about the time used for travelling to face-to-face meetings with a global group, meeting virtually clearly is less time intensive. The difference is simply that the time spent travelling is familiar to people while virtuality often feels alien. Thus the goal is for groups to familiarize themselves with working on- and offline over the distance and shape behavioural patterns based on good practice, as described above. See Chapter Eight for how to make the best use of technology to achieve this goal.

Textbox 6.2: Definition: Dimension "Global Netiquette Skills"

The degree to which members employ global netiquette (commonly accepted guidelines for virtual communication) and encourage other members to do so as well.

Item 1: The degree to which members have agreed on a common set of netiquette behaviours.

This item addresses questions like: Do common guidelines exist for members on how to communicate virtually, like writing emails, participating in conference calls, etc.? How refined are these guidelines, i.e. do they cover the use of different email features such as CC or is there an agreed procedure on how to facilitate a conference call? Is there a common understanding of how to address people or the use of emoticons (i.e. smileys) or abbreviations?

Item 2: The degree to which members utilize the commonly accepted guidelines for virtual communication and cooperation.

This item addresses questions like: Does the majority of members stick to the agreed guidelines? Do members sometimes relapse into individual or local habits? Do different rules exist within the group?

Good Practice

Global Netiquette Skills denote members' ability to implement guidelines for virtual collaboration. They are at the heart of the *How* of connecting. Successful implementation of these guidelines presupposes their acceptance by all group members. Forcing a pre-conceived netiquette onto a diverse group is not likely to work. That said, group processes can be accelerated significantly by the existence of a set of organization-wide, non-negotiable guidelines for global cooperation. These then form the basis upon which virtual groups can build their E-Culture without having to start from scratch.

Given that netiquette is defined by shared behaviours, it is an area with very contested views and practices. Is frowning considered impolite? Or interrupting? Who calls back when a call breaks down – the initial caller or the recipient? Is the email "cc" function used to include group members or as a means to escalate issues? Suffice to say at this point that creating a shared netiquette that is tailored to a group's needs is best done through a participative negotiating process among each virtual group.

Our Advice

Many groups lose a lot of time through identifying and agreeing on ground rules for virtual collaboration. They have to set up rules for media use, including all features of the different media, as well as agree on how to design decision-making processes and other important team processes such as e-meeting norms.

Taking this into account, a huge amount of time can be saved and productivity significantly improved by agreeing on a set of norms on an organizational or even company-wide level to establish a corporate E-Culture.

This could include meeting standards (for face-to-face as well as virtual meetings) such as using invitation templates or on norms for how to use different media and the corresponding functions, such as ccing in email or emoticons in a chat.

Negotiating a global netiquette is relatively easy compared to other tasks virtual groups face. It is therefore a great way to start developing the shared collaboration space.

6.5 Media Competence

Having access to technology that enables the creation of a shared collaboration space is a fundamental and non-negotiable prerequisite for virtual collaboration. Providing and using the right media for the right purpose is both a leader's responsibility and a task for organization development. On the other hand, the virtual leader also has to deal with personal preferences and individual competences regarding the use of different media, based on members' previous experiences or the local cultural context.

Virtual Closeness and the creation of a Purple Space within a virtual group can only be fostered if these individual aspects are taken into account when deciding which media to use.

Textbox 6.3: Definition: Dimension "Media Competence"

The degree to which members have access to relevant media tools and proactively employ these according to group objectives and other members' needs.

Item 1: Members have access to the same media and tools needed for communication and cooperation.

This item addresses questions like: Do different tools or different versions of the same tool co-exist in different parts of the organization? Do different Internet-line bandwidths create an imbalance in communication processes? Do all members have equal access to the same tools? Do all members have the same software versions and hardware solutions? Do all members have the relevant tools to get the job done?

Item 2: Members are flexible in their choice of media and tools depending on the tasks and the needs of other members.

This item addresses questions like: Are members aware of the various media available for virtual communication and cooperation: email, telephone, instant messenger, etc.? Are members aware of the different strengths of different applications? Are members aware of different media preferences? Do members take personal preferences and the different strengths of media into account when deciding which ones to use?

Good Practice

Media Competence is an area that exposes generational differences like no other. Like cultural learning, learning how to use media and communicate virtually is challenging because it requires a will to access and transform deeply held values. Media Competence is not only about which media are used to connect but also about group members' maturity in handling the available technology and dealing with different competence levels within the group. An intervention will start by examining whether people have access to necessary media and the skills to use them. Media Competence is discussed in more detail in Chapter Eight.

Finally, when creating Virtual Closeness in groups with individuals who possess different maturity levels of virtualization, the more mature ones also need to have high maturity levels in Media Competence, Feedback Competence, Communication Styles, and Global

Netiquette Skills. Those with lower maturity levels have to be trained and supported to grow in these areas. Indicators for maturity levels include the amount of daily work processes that are computer-based and processed remotely with the help of someone's Online Identity (see Online Identity Competence below).

Our Advice

Chapter Eight contains in-depth information and guidance on how to develop Media Competence. Here, it will suffice to give some examples that span the scope of media and technology use for virtual global groups.

✓ Less is more. This applies to the amount of media used in virtual group work. When too many communication channels are used, people may not know which ones to use and communication can quickly become inefficient. It is more productive to focus on a few and ensure that everyone has access to them and knows well how to use them. This is particularly true for virtual meeting points such as social media or project-management spaces. When too many of them are on the table, it is a bit like having ten cafeterias none of which is frequented in a way that brings people together. It is better to have one cosy cafeteria where everyone likes to come frequently.

✓ Determining which media to use for virtual group work can be a leadership task. A lot of time can be saved when the group leader makes the relevant choices at the beginning of the project. The time spent in deep negotiation processes can be saved for more critical aspects such as establishing a voicing and feedback culture or relationship building. However, these media decisions should also be based on personal and cultural preferences within the group. Moreover, media choices should always encompass formal as well as informal interaction spaces, as well as synchronous and asynchronous communication channels.

✓ When possible, training in the use of those media chosen for virtual collaboration should ideally be given in a face-to-face workshop. If that is not possible, virtual training should be delivered to the various office sites in synchronous time with face-to-face practice in local groups or tandems. Media training, while it may seem superfluous to some people, will help to overcome fears and technical hurdles in a shared and supportive manner. Practising using the technology that will accompany a virtual group throughout their collaboration time is a helpful test drive to simulate the subsequent reality. Using physical time together for that signals that Media Competence is a priority.

✓ However, kicking off a virtual-group phase should happen virtually. Contrary to widespread belief, this promises better performance than a face-to-face kick off. A virtual kick off signals that virtuality is the reality wherein a group will work. Precious face-to-face time is better saved for making important decisions and solving conflict.

✓ Voicing (see Chapter Two) is equally important regarding media and technology. Acknowledging successful media use and respectfully criticizing any misuse in good time will help the group to develop their Media Competence continuously.

✓ Establishing the shared collaboration space (the Purple Space) requires meeting as equals. This means that, rather than meeting in the web room of one part of the team ("dialling in"), all members come together in the same agreed-on purple meeting space.

➢ A global group has one member located in Finland. He was often forgotten by his far-flung co-workers. To increase his visibility, he sent a photograph of himself to his colleagues, asking them to put it up on their desks. That way, he proactively sent the message: "Remember to include me."

➢ The majority of the members of another global group are located in the same office while the other members are dispersed around the globe. The majority group transmits most of their face-to-face meetings to their remote colleagues. They either use web-conferencing technology for direct participation or they create and transmit the meeting minutes in real time through a chat or an application sharing system.

6.6 Online Identity Competence

Virtual group work relies as much on members' lived and perceived professional identities as collocated work does. In order to be visible virtually, it is vital that the individual be perceived as a human being – and able to perceive others likewise. Only real human beings with personalities can belong to a shared purple collaboration space. We call this process of leaving traces online and the perception of these cues by others 'Online Identity'. Online Identity is a matter of how someone chooses to be present when connecting with remote colleagues. Online Identity is particularly important for virtual leadership and is therefore discussed further in Chapter Seven.

Textbox 6.4: Definition: Dimension "Online Identity Competence"

The degree to which members develop an authentic online identity that helps to build and manage relationships.

Item 1: Members are aware of how they are perceived online/virtually by the other members of the group.

This item addresses questions like: Do members appreciate what their online activities say about them? To what degree are they consequently perceived as authentic human beings? What kind of professional identity is created through these virtual clues? Will there be unexpected surprises when people meet face-to-face or will there be a feeling of familiarity?

Item 2: Members are able to build and manage relationships in online/virtual contexts.

This item addresses questions like: How do members create trust when they do not meet face-to-face? How do members know the feelings of their communication partner when they only read emails from her or him? Do they know how their messages are perceived by others? Are they able to transport the strengths they have in face-to-face communication into the virtual world?

Good Practice

During the 1990s, we analyzed a series of text-based, virtual conferences in order to identify:

- The characteristic dimensions of an online-identity, and

- The success factors for professional relationship management in the virtual world.

To that end, we identified and classified a large sample of text-based contributions from discussion forums that had a high impact on the respective virtual groups, either provoking a lot of interaction or muting discussions. The results we found basically coincide with the concepts of Schweizer et al. (2002) (social presence) and of Garrison et al. (2000) (cognitive presence and leadership presence).

Social Presence, Cognitive Presence, and Leadership Presence

A person's Online Identity is shaped by three types of virtual presence: social presence, leadership presence, and cognitive presence.

Figure 6.1: Online Identity

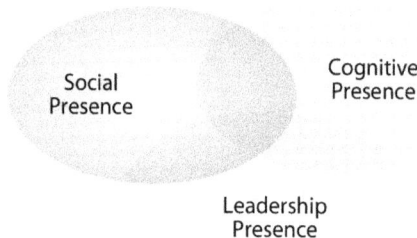

Social Presence

The most important aspect of an Online Identity is being perceived as a human being when online. In absence of such a perception, it is very easy for others to ignore an individual's messages or just delete them. When a manager opens her email inbox in the morning, the first decision of the day is, "Who will I disappoint today by not responding to their email?", given that there are generally more messages than one person can manage to reply to in one day.

Here is where Virtual Closeness comes in. If a message is identified as being from someone the recipient has a functioning relationship with and perceives as an authentic human being, it will rank higher on the list of priorities than others.

After all, when entering a colleague's office intending to ask him to perform a certain task, a good manager won't just open the door and say, "Do this task." He would instead search for social cues from the other, grounded in the context of their relationship, in order to get a collaborative response. While individual behaviour may vary depending on the cultural context and the situation, there will usually be social cues signalling readiness or aversion. Such cues are conceptualized by the notion of social presence[1]:

> *Social presence is defined by the degree to which the partner of interaction is perceived as a person (in a virtual room).*

In virtual interaction, both in synchronous and asynchronous settings, social presence manifests itself in three ways, as can be seen, for example, in a text-based discussion forum[2]:

- Affective responses: emoticons, humor, self-revelation
- Cohesive responses: exclamations and greetings, addressing the group with "we", "our" or "us"
- Interactive responses: using "reply features", direct quotation, referring explicitly to contents of other messages.

These phenomena apply to all other virtual ways of interaction, both in synchronous and asynchronous settings, and are not limited to text-based communication. The following textbox contains good practice, which we have collected and created in our consulting processes.

Textbox 6.5: Creating Social Presence in a Phone Conference

In a phone conference, social presence can be created with the following measures:

- Start a telephone conference with a round of human-interest stories, which can be designed in a number of ways. One example includes every member sharing a statement about his or her current personal or professional situation. Or members could share gossip about what's going on in their respective locations. The point is to start with an exchange of informal rather than formal information in order to warm up. What is everyone's current context, including cultural aspects such as holidays? What's the weather like?
- End with rounds of members giving each other feedback, on what has been presented during the meeting or on other current work.
- Structure a meeting and simulate reality by using a team clock and/or avatars. If 3D technology isn't available yet, having the images of members' avatars visible for everyone is a good way of creating social presence.
- Don't present substantial data and facts during a teleconference – they can be read before or after. Do, however, market the data and information that demand action. Offer data to catch the others' attention.
- Use storytelling to promote data and facts, for example with success stories.
- In each virtual meeting, ask one member to tell the others more about his or her professional and personal life (and another member in the next meeting etc.). Address birthdays and/or local traditions and holidays.

If social presence underlies successful relationship management, successful task orientation presupposes the existence of cognitive presence.

Cognitive Presence

Virtual communication demands that messages be made even more precise and understandable than they are in face-to-face settings, where spontaneous responses are possible in physical interaction and the communication partner's facial and bodily expressions signal her understanding or lack thereof, her approval or disapproval. Without the communicative comfort of physical presence, such implied understanding is much more challenging in the virtual world, especially when intercultural aspects come into play. Take, for example, the wide variety of potential meanings that can be attached to smiles. The Thai know more than a dozen different ways to smile, only a few of which are recognizable to Western perception[3]. In the West as well, we often find minuscule differences or nuances, which might charge a "smile" with a different meaning. Ask yourself: how is it that, within your cultural frame, you are able to distinguish between an affectionate and an ironic smile? One of the most frequent assessments of US American smiles from a German perspective is that they are fake.

Garrison and Anderson[4] have introduced the concept of cognitive presence in the context of learning settings. We propose to extend their definition to business contexts:

> *Cognitive presence is the extent to which people are able to construct meaning and knowledge in the framework of a process of reflection and communication (in a virtual room).*

Textbox 6.6: Indicators for Cognitive Presence

Indicators for cognitive presence include the following actions in the communicative routine of a virtual group:

- Problems and surprises are expressed
- Information is exchanged
- Suggestions are made
- Brainstorming takes place
- Syntheses are suggested
- Summaries are made
- Applications are discussed
- Insight is gained from arguments and conflict.

From: Garrison, D.R. and Terry Anderson, *E-Learning in the 21ˢᵗ Century: A Framework for Research and Practice*, RoutledgeFalmer: London, 2003

Leadership Presence

Leadership presence complements social and cognitive presence in that it describes how these two aspects are implemented and balanced by a leader in the virtual context. Anderson et al. discuss this aspect in the context of learning and call it "teaching presence"[5]. We have adapted their approach to leadership and suggest the following definition.

> *Leadership presence is defined as the design, moderation and organization of cognitive and social processes (in virtual rooms) with the purpose of achieving results.*

To display leadership presence, a person will proactively create and facilitate the cultural and technological framework wherein a group can interact. This interaction is characterized by social and cognitive presence, role modelled by the leader. In her interactions with employees, she will manage relationships and work tasks, thereby serving as an example that will be imitated by group members. Keep in mind that negative behaviour is copied as quickly as positive behaviour and can undermine group cohesion and impact group dynamics strongly. It is therefore crucial that the leader know how the three types of presence are created and displayed.

Textbox 6.7: Indicators for Leadership Presence

A widespread leadership task in virtuality is e-moderation or e-coaching. Typical indicators for leadership presence marshalled by the moderator or coach include:

- Identifying areas of agreement/discourse
- Seeking to reach consensus and/or foster understanding
- Encouraging, acknowledging, or reinforcing team contributions
- Setting a climate for learning
- Drawing in participants, promoting discussion
- Assessing process efficiency.

From: Garrison, D.R. and Terry Anderson, *E-Learning in the 21ˢᵗ Century: A Framework for Research and Practice*, RoutledgeFalmer: London, 2003

The right amount and mix of social and cognitive presence depends on the media used and on the individual and cultural context. A very long email may contain plenty of social presence cues but may not be received too well by the reader due to its overwhelming length. Moreover, the cultural context determines the balance. An email from a Mexican marketing expert may be filled with more social presence than one written by a German engineer. However, there should always be some elements of social presence in any act of communication, independent of the medium – or alternatively, an absence of social presence should be explicitly compensated for in another medium.

Our experience has further given rise to an important observation. There is a slight shift in the way a person is regarded as an authority in the virtual world as opposed to in non-virtual communication. As there are generally less personal cues transported in a virtual communication process, descriptions such as "charisma" and "influential presenter or speaker" often lose meaning in predominantly text-based interaction. In virtuality, the level of being perceived as an authority is more intimately linked to knowledge and expertise (cognitive presence) than in face-to-face collaboration. A leader who mainly focuses on process facilitation without contributing sufficient expertise to problem solving might not be considered an authority. Consequently, process facilitation and moderation skills[6] as a source for asserting leadership presence do not automatically work in a text-based asynchronous environment. This kind of leadership works better in synchronous, voice-based interactions.

Our Advice

A useful way of working on group members' Online Identity is to analyze their emails, chat entries, or wiki entries in terms of social, cognitive, and leadership presence and to give feedback on how each other's Communication Styles are perceived.

Showing social presence online – making oneself visible – becomes easier when informal communication channels are made available in addition to formal ones. When using Skype, for example, selecting the green "Online" symbol signals more social presence than always selecting "Not available" or "Invisible". This applies also to the leader. When she regularly chooses not to be visibly available online, this is similar to a leader who doesn't come to the office.

A leader can decide to have availability times. Once a week, for example, he could be on WebEx during fixed hours. Every group member can reach him and talk to him. If nobody shows up during the online office hours, that is ok, too. It is about clearly signalling presence and availability. A leader could also increase her presence by writing a blog to share her thoughts and ideas with all group members. This is also another great way to reduce email. Blog content must be interesting to group members, though.

Another way of increasing social (online) presence is by spending breaks together. This could mean taking one's laptop to the coffee machine so that colleagues can be there (e.g. on Skype) or playing online Wii.

> ➢ The above vignette of the Finnish group member is a good example of showing social presence. When we don't see our colleagues, we might only perceive their cognitive presence through the project work. Social presence requires a visual element like his photograph or an avatar representing this person in a way that links his or her personality with traits of the avatar. Most of us rely on our vision to build relationships and feel close to other people.

6.7 Self Reflection: Lessons Learned from Chapter Six: "Is It Honne?": Finding and Applying VPI Dimensions in the Story

In this part of Chapter Six, we provide you with a guided tour to reflect potential learning about the category "E-Culture" and its corresponding four dimensions (Global Netiquette Skills, Media Competence, Online Identity Competence, and Virtual Experiences), based on elements of our story.

One of the key concerns for professionals communicating virtually is the question of how they are to transport their competences and presence online (Online Identity). This notion is often especially strong with members that have come to virtual communication relatively late in their lives, like Kenji Sakamoto. While his son is a "digital native" designing avatars in California, Sakamoto struggles with several of the VPI dimensions at once.

First of all, he is lacking *Virtual Experiences*.

Two weeks ago, Hui Yuan gave him a one-on-one introduction to the media used in the team. He was embarrassed about his first attempts at using the Internet, but he never really needed it for his production job at Beltronik.

Secondly, Sakamoto lacks *Media Competence*.

The young Chinese has sent him another chat message, as he calls it. At least he notices the messages now. Until recently, because he didn't know that his computer has this function, his chat window was always closed.

Please consider the following: If you would be a leader of a virtual group, how could you ensure that the necessary skills are developed in the group for all members to feel competent and thus close to the media used? How could those that have a lot of Virtual Experience support those with less? How could you pay respect to personal or cultural media preferences?

Thirdly, Sakamoto has strong doubts about whether he can develop an *Online Identity* that adequately conveys his authority and personality.

Another issue is that in virtuality, he comes across like a ghost. "Honne", one's true voice, is not audible. Only "tatemae", one's façade, makes an appearance. Some people call this a lack of authenticity. To him it means that being oneself comes less naturally. After twenty years of supervising others, a certain way of being silent or the movement of an eyebrow can send messages to his co-workers and colleagues in a way that words could not. Can he change this? Does he want to change this? Perhaps he ought to talk about this to Gupta, who has a decent age and, unlike himself, moves between the worlds.

Whether members feel virtually close to a group, its members, and its purpose depends to a large degree on whether they feel they can be who and as they are. This can be especially challenging for people from organizational or country cultures where leadership is very much based on personal contact and/or charisma.

Consider for a moment: How could you as a group leader support members to develop their full potential in collaborating online? Is there something that might even be gained while reflecting and establishing an authentic virtual presence and how might you use that to make the virtual working space even more attractive and turn it into a Purple Space? How can the virtual enable us to transcend boundaries of gender, ethnicity, age, and culture?

While authenticity is important for creating Virtual Closeness, it is not enough to create a professional Online Identity. Group members also have to show social and cognitive presence.

Sakamoto identifies a sign for an improved cognitive presence on the part of the different group members when he thinks that *they are now making an effort to use simple English. This indicates that other group members try to make the content of their messages easier to understand.* And by using so many emoticons, Yuan has a strong social presence.

> Do you find further traces of social presence, however small, in this part of the story? Personal self-disclosure, for example.

Global Netiquette Skills

All three dimensions of E-Culture discussed until now directly connect with the fourth – Global Netiquette Skills, the ability to negotiate and agree upon common communication rules in virtual communication and to stick to them.

Hui Yuan's message is still blinking on the screen. It reads, "Move into new apt. on Friday. Wife \^o^/."

He is doing it again! Yuan constantly includes symbols that he doesn't understand. And the longer they know each other, the more symbols he uses. It had started with the symbol (^_^)? ... How should he deal with this in the future? The Brazilian and the American also used symbols that his grandchildren, however, had not seen before.

> Please ask yourself: How could you as a group leader initiate a netiquette process? When would be a good time to start it? What might be potential challenges? How can you ensure that the agreements include all members? How can netiquette, potentially combined with humour, help develop a sense of Virtual Closeness? How could you use the netiquette as a building block to develop a joint Purple Space?

Beyond agreeing on the question of which media to use for which purpose, there are other potential factors involved.

Which other elements might potentially be included in a netiquette process? How, later on, can you monitor the agreements? How can you motivate members to support the netiquette? What do you do when you notice breeches in the netiquette? What do you do when you notice that others notice breeches in the netiquette but do nothing about it? What role can "voicing" play in the process?

After having analyzed the facets of the four dimensions for virtual performance improvement in the category "E-Culture" in at least one example, we invite you to continue screening the story for further clues on the dimensions of Global Netiquette Skills, Media Competence, Online Identity Competence, and Virtual Experiences.

Having collected more "data", imagine being the leader of this team or an external consultant and ask yourself the following questions:

What would you like to improve and why?
What could be a measure to improve the virtual performance of this group?
How would you bring the topic(s) into the group?
How would you work on it/them?
How would you monitor it/them?
How would you keep the topic(s) alive?

Your Notes

6.8 Coaching Questions for E-Culture

Start with the following questions:

- What is your understanding of the category "E-Culture"?
  (If needed, it would be good to give some input on "E-Culture".)
- How would you describe the present situation in the group?
- Could you please describe the degree of access to different communication technologies in the locations involved?
- Which tools do you proactively use and which not?
- Why do you choose some above others?
- Do all members have the same media access?
- How often does your group connect and how?
- How do you think the members would describe the e-communication situation?
- What are your "hopes/wishes/plans" for the group in the future regarding this?

Global Netiquette Skills

- What is your understanding of "Global Netiquette Skills"?
- What do you think is necessary for a good virtual interaction?
- Please describe how the members behave in/with different media.
- Does your group have a shared understanding of the way to communicate in the different media? If yes, what does it look like? If no, why not?

Media Competence

- Please describe the media that are available.
- Are the media available in all locations?
- How stable are the connections (Internet etc.)?
- Please describe the media that you use in the team.
- What do you use the media for?
- Do you use media for social interaction? If yes, which media?

Online Identity Competence

- Please go through the following for each member:
    - How "digitally native" is each member (how familiar are they with digital communication)?
    - Do you have social interaction in virtual spaces?
- Are there members that you feel closer to than to others?
- What do these members do differently compared to the other members?

Virtual Experiences

- Please go through the following for each member:
    - How experienced is each member in working virtually?
    - What do these members do differently compared to the other members?
    - What would those that are less experienced need to feel more comfortable?
- Which kind of training or support was offered to strengthen the members' ability to handle different media?

Notes

1 Schweizer et al. (2002).
2 Ibid.
3 Wyatt (2003).
4 Garrison and Anderson (2003).
5 Garrison et al. (2000); Anderson et al. (2001).
6 Facilitation is a result-open approach to the support of groups in the context of interactions such as discussions. Moderation is the support of groups in interactions such as discussions that is aimed at achieving an externally set goal (for example, teachers are usually moderators, not facilitators). For e-moderation, see Salmon (2004).

● ●

Where Do We Go From Here?

Initially, Moser had wanted to join him in Dubai but had to cancel the day before their departure because he had come down with the flu. The appointment in Dubai was important as the investors at "The Light" had started to show a deeper interest in the Global Virtual Quality Circle's work. The reason for this was probably that the comprehensive changes and the introduction of a matrix structure had resulted in a deteriorated, rather than improved, overall corporate financial performance.

Against this background, every piece of good news was welcome, particularly when it contained the possibility of improving international cooperation and, with it, the company's performance. Bell had offered Moser the opportunity to join the meeting via video or WebEx.

"The benefit of virtual collaboration is that there is no risk of infection, at least physically. And you can still take credit for the project vis-à-vis our stakeholders…" But Moser had just grunted and not really reacted to his ironic-buoyant invitation. His supervisor must indeed have been really sick.

Bell is now landing in Dubai for the fourth time in three months. Since his local team has developed well, he needn't be there physically too often. His wife, Britta, is also happy about that. Once the family went to Dubai together for a long weekend and Britta had been bored to death after only eight hours. Luckily, his sons had abandoned the ego-shooter games ever since Sakamoto-san started sending them Mangas from Japan every month.

While the plane is taxiing towards the terminal, he watches the Arabian night unfold outside. No stars, just the orange smearing caused by light pollution. But no sandstorm either – things have calmed and his thoughts have cleared. While his other areas of responsibility continue to undergo constant changes, the Global Virtual Quality Circle has been producing fruitful results over the past months, first and foremost because the members have embarked on a joint learning journey.

This hasn't always been easy. In the beginning, intercultural misunderstandings, above all, led to miscommunication. But the team was also struggling with different

Work Styles, completely differing perspectives on feedback, and how to handle hierarchies or delegate tasks.

The Asians had felt cut off from the flow of information, which had impacted their motivation. While a common workflow was established relatively fast, the team was often struggling with a lack of organizational support for their project work. Also, while all of them seemed to be overwhelmed by their workload, different coping strategies surfaced. Britt from Sweden kept repeating "We need to learn to say no" like a mantra.

The team experienced a real breakthrough when they realized that the geographical distance between them actually had quite a few advantages. Patricia, for example, was able to work from her chosen location (otherwise the company would have lost her) and team performance profited from the "follow the sun" principle. Challenges appeared when they did not spend enough time in shared dialogue. This often resulted in a lack of visibility of single members' contributions, which in turn raised doubts about whether the workload was distributed evenly.

While some of the Europeans had worked together before, thus bringing social capital, as Ranjit called it, to the team, the Asians and Paolo felt rather cut off from the core team in the beginning. Because of this, they sometimes didn't share information as openly as Bell had hoped. It also became clear that he should have forged a stronger identification with the project among team members. Instead, identification developed through the sympathy people felt for each other – not a generally reliable feature of business relations, though. In addition, language issues arose during the first weeks of the project because some members dominated the team's communication due to language or cultural reasons.

Sakamoto-san's and Hui Yuan's feelings of being excluded were compounded by their lack of Virtual Experiences. A number of members, including himself, were also concerned about being authentic in the virtual context. How he had envied his sons their playful ability to adopt a variety of online identities! It soon became clear that the differing use of the available media called for negotiating an online etiquette among team members.

They can now pass these experiences on to other teams and departments as structured recommendations. That alone was worth the investment in the Global Virtual Quality Circle.

The plane is docking at the gate. Some passengers start hauling their oversized hand luggage from the overhead compartments. How he hates these moments of pushing to the exit, something entirely absent from virtual travel. In a few hours, he'll be in Abu Salama's office. Salama will offer him tea (99 per cent probability), thank him for his work (95 per cent probability), listen to him carefully, and ask him (100 per cent probability), "Ah Florian, my friend, where do we go from here?"

●●●

CHAPTER SEVEN

Selected Aspects of Virtual Leadership

7.1   The Virtual Leader

7.2   Voicing

7.3   Attractiveness

7.4   Negotiation Processes: Creating Purple (Collaboration) Spaces

7.5   Leadership Presence: Availability and Visibility of the Virtual Leader

7.6   Managing the Links

This chapter is intended to touch only on selected aspects of virtual leadership as they relate to the 20 dimensions of the Virtual Performance Improvement. The leadership of virtual teams, groups, and networks is a complex topic and invaluable work has been done on it[1]. As we are in the process of developing a specialized VPA tool for virtual leadership, we intend to offer an exhaustive discussion of the topic in a subsequent publication.

7.1 The Virtual Leader

Imagine the virtual leader as a pilot sitting in his cockpit with 20 items on his control panel for flying the plane. From his cockpit he is reacting to influences such as weather, day or night light levels, and air traffic. Even when on autopilot, he will have an eye on the control panel at all times to ensure smooth and effective cruising.

In this metaphor, the 20 devices on the control panel represent the 20 VPI dimensions that you know from the previous five chapters. They are interrelated. If one changes, others are bound to be influenced as well. The virtual leader's job is to focus on the entirety of those 20 dimensions and work within them selectively and systematically, together with his group. You can also think of the 20 VPI dimensions as gears that can be adjusted individually in order to affect a situation.

Every larger organization today is based on virtual collaboration with differing degrees of the use of virtuality. The virtually operating organization is often a matrix or a network structure that demands different and additional management skills. We have met many managers in global virtual environments who find it difficult to live up to the requirements. Why? Because the leaders and managers[2] in most organizations are still trained following traditional principles of organizational forms that are mainly manager centred and based on the belief that organizations can be steered with predictable cause-and-effect mechanisms. Both principles work in virtual organizations only to a limited extent.

In our experience, once a manager or leader understands that she is not or no longer heading a traditional group that is characterized by job descriptions, hierarchy, power dynamics, and control, but rather a matrix or a network, she opens up to learning the skills and acquiring the wisdom necessary to lead effectively in that environment. The successful leader of the future will be a network person leading and managing in a virtual environment with increasing network components and degrees of self-organization and Shared Leadership.

"If only we had clear roles and responsibilities, or if only the processes were clearly defined, everything would be better", we often hear managers sigh. Unfortunately, this is an illusion that might indicate where leadership thinking has to change.

Many people working in networks fill several roles at the same time. They may be part of a virtual group, directly reporting to someone located elsewhere. They may participate in other projects simultaneously. Being a member of a temporary or sustained network organization or community means coping with being part of a number of different projects and fulfilling a number of different tasks throughout the day whilst having little or no power in the traditional sense. In this way, roles and responsibilities and the balance between information push and pull might have to be adjusted even on a self-organized and situational basis. Naturally, we will invest ourselves most comprehensively in the context we feel closest to, usually that from which we receive the most benefits. Such investments are signs of Virtual Closeness and the existence of Purple Space.

At core, these challenges are leadership issues. If the leader doesn't manage to encourage and support the building of a shared collaboration space with reduced complexity (the Purple Space) through authenticity, inclusive communication, and conflict management, members will not 'log on' or quickly 'log off'. While a process aiming at the development of a Purple Space creates orderly structure, the glue that holds this structure together is the feeling of the people involved that they are important to the process – and vice versa. Fluent, vivid, and creative by nature, network or virtual organizations and communities are characterized by high levels of ambivalence. Due to the breakdown of the classical leadership principles of steering and predictability, leaders in nonlinear systems have to be able to cope with high degrees of uncertainty and ambiguity, which can be quite unsettling. In virtual groups, this is particularly acute given that leaders and managers are often not available physically, thus exerting less direct power. They are challenged to find alternative ways of endorsing working relationships and supporting a group atmosphere that makes members want to participate.

> A person leading a virtual group that is spread out globally from his Paris location has established a good practice of virtual leadership that has supported his group members to feel virtually close to each other. In addition to the formal online platforms used for the project work, he opened a chat room for the personal

exchanges amongst members. They log into that chat room first thing in the morning to greet their colleagues and chitchat about their weekend, evening, or the like. The chat room remains active throughout the working day as informal information is shared – just as it would be during lunch or coffee in a collocated office. The high level of participation shows that members feel that they belong to the group (Virtual Closeness) and that they have a shared Purple Space where they can interact independently from their own location. The leader himself also uses the informal channel actively, both to discuss business-related topics and to show social presence. He regularly encourages his co-workers to make frequent and active use of the chat room to reduce email correspondence.

In the absence of that crucial sense of participation, ownership, commitment, obligation, and purpose, people will bypass the process to find their own way through the system, just as water flows in the direction which allows it to meet the fewest obstacles. When this happens, virtual groups face a phenomenon that Pateau Consultants have called "friendly avoidance mode"[3]. In the friendly avoidance mode, group members pretend to be getting along well whilst really avoiding one another, not reacting to the others' needs. When asked by the leader to do something that they don't support or understand, they are likely to pretend to do it in order to avoid open conflict. The strengths of virtual leaders must therefore lie in enabling, mediating, facilitating, and moderating communication, feedback, and conflict. They should also continuously negotiate with all group members a customized virtual collaboration culture that leads to reduced complexity. That way, the leader sets and guards the framework (the Purple Space) wherein virtual collaboration takes place.

Based on the above description and on our extensive experience of working with large global organizations, we have identified five key aspects (in addition to classical leadership tasks and Shared Leadership as a general success factor) that the virtual leader needs to take into account to focus on and accomplish his or her work:

- ✓ Voicing

- ✓ Attractiveness

✓ Negotiation

✓ Availability

✓ Links.

Let us now examine these five building blocks of virtual leadership in the context of VPI.

7.2 Voicing

Before a virtual group can even begin to improve its performance through working on most of the 20 VPI dimensions, its members need to be able to communicate with each other virtually. Establishing a healthy voicing culture is therefore the first task for the virtual leader. The concept of voicing has already been introduced in Chapter Two in the context of the dimension Feedback Competence.

We often hear virtual leaders say, "Everything is going well in my group because I hardly hear anything from them". Unfortunately, many leaders of virtual groups believe that the absence of conflict and criticism is a good sign. In reality, the opposite is true. The absence of outspoken conflict often points to a state of friendly avoidance of other people or situations. In a virtual context, politely ignoring one another is much easier than in collocated settings.

Addressing a group's "hot topics" without having a shared culture of voicing important issues in place is very difficult. A voicing culture is also the basis for negotiating the norms of interacting in the Purple Space. It is a continuous process of actively searching for weak signals of disagreement and building on them.

Feedback, on the other hand, builds on this ability and willingness to voice. However, feedback usually focuses on the behaviour of others and is intended to initiate a behavioural change as desired by the feedback giver. In being a more open process and touching also on abstract organizational issues, voicing is therefore more general than feedback. That said, we are using the concepts of voicing and feedback interchangeably as together they form a specific group culture.

In virtual settings, people can choose to avoid the other entirely. In the absence of talking to each other and voicing critical issues, problems can quickly grow out of proportion and lead to inertia. A state of fake tolerance – not tolerating the other's behaviour but not voicing it – is created. In the below image of the "Tolerance Traffic Light", fake tolerance is represented by the yellow circle[4].

Figure 7.1: The Tolerance Traffic Light

Fake tolerance is a dangerous state for a group that can result in a spiral of miscommunication (see Chapter Two, page 47). A lack of the voicing of one's concerns is one reason for underperformance. Conversely, establishing a culture of voicing is one of the most successful ways of creating high performance.

> *Voicing is a culture of professional spontaneous and continuous response in the face-to-face and virtual workplace.*

In order to get the most out of the complexity and cultural diversity of a global group, a high level of voicing and Feedback Competence on the part of all members is essential. Feedback as a crucial leadership competence is necessary in order to raise critical and positive aspects of cooperation as well as awareness of work and Communication Styles and shared responsibility among all group members.

See also Chapter Two for more information on voicing.

Recommendations for Virtual Leaders

✓ Start to create and implement a voicing culture from the beginning. Be a role model! Practise what you preach. Show your group members how voicing works in face-to-face and virtual settings and that it is ok if they articulate their concerns in a respectful and productive, culturally compatible way[5].

✓ Voicing and behaviour-based feedback should generally be done in three modes:
  • *Continue* – more of this!
  • *Start* – you are doing fine but please do or show more of x, y, or z.
  • *Stop* – no more!

✓ Through establishing a voicing culture, you are simultaneously building your group's Purple Space. Make sure to invest sufficient time in understanding what works for your group and what doesn't when it comes to voicing and giving feedback. Less is more in this context as it leads to reduced complexity. Remember that it is your job to include the different cultural preferences into the new and shared group culture you are building with your colleagues.

✓ Establish voicing as a permanent agenda item. In order to grow, your group needs to reflect on their practice of discussing their communication, voicing and giving feedback. Your role is to facilitate this continuous reflection of what did or did not work.

✓ Ideally, an organization commits to building a global voicing culture so that all members in all geographical locations can base their communication on shared principles.

➢ One of our clients, an international online-platform provider, has implemented a global voicing culture. This is the first training new employees get. In that training, participants train voicing through hands-on, experiential learning by practising, *inter alia*, the continue–start–stop model (see above).

7.3 Attractiveness

Another key principle of virtual leadership is attractiveness. With increasing attractiveness of a particular people- or work-related context, energy and information follow the pull rather than the push principle. People are pulled towards a group, a network, or a community and bring with them information and expertise. Pushing information in their direction in order to get their buy-in becomes more or less unnecessary.

Virtual leadership does not function according to traditional power dynamics. Because virtuality allows people to ignore a leader who doesn't live up to what members need from him, the principles of power and hierarchy generally don't apply. In the absence of coercion and control, motivation and performance are fuelled by the degree of attractiveness an organization or a group can develop and emanate to the individual leader or employee. People will join and stay when they find it attractive to be a part of the organization or group, for a variety of individual reasons that are similar to why people join social movements or follow fashion.

Whereas traditional organizations operate hierarchically, are manager-centred, and base their internal authority on power and control, the above principles apply chiefly to globally and virtually operating organizations that can usually be categorized somewhere between a matrix and a network organization. Matrixes and networks are characterized by group work, situational coupling of competences, and employee creativity. Most of those organizations, particularly the bigger ones, have features of both forms. Some departments may be organized as a matrix while others have clear network features.

> ➢ When a group is attractive enough, participants will come to it. There is a recurring phenomenon in talent and trainee programs. Future participants often connect with each other on virtual platforms even before the programs start. The reason is the attractiveness of such intra-organizational social networks, both for personal and for career reasons.

Attractiveness has to be considered on two levels of organizational life: the personal and the organizational.

Attractiveness on the Personal Level

To better understand the principle of attractiveness, consider this example from family life. A mother is often travelling for work. When away, she talks to her teenage daughter several times a day on Skype.

When she isn't behaving in a way that actually makes her daughter want to talk to her, the girl will simply go offline, particularly when she feels pressured by the mother. The same is true for working groups. When the virtual leader doesn't let people know she values them and their work and merely exercises pressure and control instead, they will go offline, metaphorically and actually. This is the phenomenon of friendly avoidance.

Attractiveness on the Organizational Level

When business areas are globalized (i.e. standardized on a global scale), the local systems and practices must often be deconstructed in favour of the new global ones. This often creates a lot of pressure for local employees. From the perspective of attractiveness, a conflict of interest arises for the organization. On the one hand, it has to go global in order to grow and reduce complexity; on the other, this process can be very unattractive for the people involved. The organization is bound to fail if it doesn't succeed in creating enough attractiveness for members to engage in the global processes.

Recommendations for Virtual Leaders

✓ Always review what makes your group and project attractive to the individual members and the organization to create high Organizational Relevance. Are they motivated to be there? If not, what can you do to regain their commitment? Attractiveness on the personal level can be created by specific incentives, including the following:
   - Personal development
   - Career development
   - Empowerment and self-organization/autonomy
   - Visibility in the organization
   - Interest in the topic
   - Learning opportunities and challenges
   - New ways and places of working together
   - Travelling options and interesting intercultural encounters
   - Private reasons.

✓ One of the keys to virtual leadership and attractiveness is Shared Leadership (Chapter Two). Often, leaders tend to exercise too much control and guidance, which can de-motivate many employees. Practising Shared Leadership requires the leader to let go of control and share her responsibility with her colleagues. That means she also needs to be comfortable with dealing with the unknown. The resulting freedom creates attractiveness and motivates employees.

✓ During globalizing and standardizing processes, make sure to also lead the local people who are impacted by the process. You can either lead them directly or work with a local leader. The key is to decide what remains local and what goes global, and to initiate a dialogue about that decision. Be aware that globalization and standardization processes are probably not very attractive for them because they are forced to give up well-establishes local practices. It is therefore important to market the benefits of the global in the local context. However, avoid devaluating former behaviour ("The new way of working together is better than the old one...").

7.4 Negotiation Processes: Creating Purple (Collaboration) Spaces

One of the main leadership challenges in a global context is the decision about which initiatives, processes, or approaches in an organization should be carried out:

• Locally (safety regulations based on the practice of the country with the highest standards, for example);

• Interculturally (deciding not only to translate important documents into other languages relevant to the organization but also to adapt them to the respective local cultures); or

• By implementing an approach that is based on getting the best out of all different relevant perspectives, leading to our concept of Purple Space. This is often called a transcultural approach; however, we do not like to use this term as its meaning refers, in fact, not just to cultural concerns but also encompasses organizational as well as technical facets.

When jointly developing a Purple Space wherein a virtual group can collaborate, the virtual leader needs highly developed negotiation skills in order to help the group agree on a shared approach.

Group members usually already belong to a local interaction space encompassing elements such as a local working and communication culture; local rules, processes, and organizational structures; local technology; and local people to whom they might feel more or less close. One member may join from a "blue" space, another from a "red" space.

The Purple Space needs to be filled with a mutual understanding of communication, voicing, processes, working schedule, and so on. Almost all of the 20 VPA dimensions can be negotiated with the whole group in order to establish a set of shared norms or shared behaviours and tools that frame the Purple Space. Developing those constituting elements (partly) together shapes the Purple Space and creates a feeling of belonging.

Negotiation is a science in and of itself and the virtual leader must master it, just as he needs to be good at facilitation and moderation. Negotiation is an essential skill of the virtual leader. Without it, the diversity in a group cannot be included and capitalized on for the purpose of high group performance.

Recommendations for Virtual Leaders

When negotiating any of the 20 VPA dimensions with your group, we recommend you do so according to the following six steps. You may already be familiar with them from the learning sections addressing our story at the end of each of chapters Two to Six.

The approach to Deep Democracy presented here is informed by the following three bodies of work: Arnold Mindell's concept of "Deep Democracy"[6]; Dorothea Schütze's and Marcus Hildebrandt's work on democratic organization development, particularly on the practice of Round Table Group Negotiation Processes in educational systems[7]; and Myrna Lewis's work, particularly her concept of "hunting for the No"[8].

The following steps and their application to an example case illustrate the Deep Democracy negotiation process.

Textbox 7.1: Steps in Deep Democracy Negotiations

1. Check: What would you like to improve and why?
2. Prepare evaluation: Identify indicators for measuring the improvement of virtual performance.
3. Reflect: How would you bring the topic(s) into the group?
4. Facilitate a process according to the following success factors:
   - *Collect all views and/or identify all involved interests, good practice, or wishes*
   - *Hunt for the "No" and/or the alternative views by identifying weak signals or areas of disagreement*
   - *Spread the "No" and/or the alternative view and/or the weak signal and add minority wisdom*
   - *Say sorry if it is not possible to fulfil the needs and/or ask "What do you need?"*
5. Plan in advance: How would you keep the topic(s) alive?
6. Use indicators transparently: How would you monitor the topic(s)?

➢ An international insurance company is globalizing its human-resources processes, particularly the compensation schemes. This process has caused numerous conflict situations for the global HR group which is tasked with implementing the changes. One of the main reasons for this is that the medium the group uses for its online communication does not have a video function. Because members can't see each other when interacting in their bi-weekly meetings, it is easy for them to "hide" and avoid true engagement with each other. That, coupled with the conflict potential of the change process, has led the group manager to initiate the following six steps.

1. *Check: What would you like to improve and why?*

When embarking on a performance-improvement process, the reason for it should be clear. The goal for any investment in organization and personnel development ought to be adding real value. Before an organization decides to globalize a business line or a specific business process (like Human Resources), it needs to be clear about the reasons for such a move and where actual value is to be added.

➤ The group manager would like to optimize the bi-weekly group meetings. Her goal is to encourage stronger virtual collaboration between group members. To that end, she wants to improve the media by adding a video function. She hopes that such a change will increase the quality and quantity of interaction and lead to more Virtual Closeness within the global HR group as a basis for a more efficient change-management process.

2. *Prepare evaluation: Identify indicators for measuring the improvement of virtual performance*

Virtual performance improvement, like any change or group-development process, ought to be measured in order to establish whether actual progress has been made. This includes an assessment of virtual leadership. The main challenge in evaluating an intangible process like organization or personnel development often lies in finding appropriate indicators. These will differ according to the individual situation of a group or an organization. However, there are some universal elements determining an evaluation. What is the framework within a virtual leader can act? This framework will be determined by contractual limitations and organizational goals that must be taken into account in the evaluation process and communicated clearly at the beginning of an improvement process.

➤ The success of the change process will be measured by increased meeting activity. Relevant indicators could include: 1. All members can see each other online. 2. All members can simultaneously see the document that is being discussed. 3. Members share more time in dialogue (or experience improvement in other VPA dimensions such as Feedback Competence, Media Competence, etc.).

3. *Reflect: How would you bring the topic(s) into the group?*

The critical "hot spots" of a virtual group as identified by the Virtual Performance Assessment indicate the areas in which the group needs to improve. For a leader, it is not always easy to address critical topics. Nonetheless, the virtual leader should name them directly (see voicing culture and Feedback Competence above and in Chapter Two) and explain why it is crucial that the group work on them. Tying these reasons to the organization's goals or values creates credibility and urgency. The leader must keep his focus on the goals and objectives for an improvement process at all times and set the process framework accordingly. The change process takes place within that frame and is binding for everyone involved.

> ➢ The manager communicates directly that she would like to improve the meeting activity. She explains that meetings shall be transformed from informational into collaborative events. She names the challenge as the need to think mutually about how to reform the group's meeting design and culture.

Another way to inject the topic into the group is the "pull" approach (if culturally applicable) which works by letting the group assess the meeting culture with respect to its objectives and its productivity and then interpret the results jointly to identify the hot spots.

4. ***Facilitate a process according to the following success factors***

This is the step where the actual negotiation takes place. We believe that the best way to create common ground while including diversity is through a process of Deep Democracy. Deeply democratic processes follow these actions:

- ▪ *Collect all views and/or identify all involved interests, good practice, or wishes:*

This is particularly important (and, at the same time, difficult) in diverse groups with a variety of different cultures or personal preferences. Work Styles, Communication Styles, and Feedback Competence are areas where views are likely to differ strongly. Collecting and explaining these different views; providing the necessary context (perspectives, personal preferences, good practices, no-nos, etc.) for everyone to be aware of the diversity in the group; and gathering good practice to build on are a necessary first step.

> ➢ The manager collects the views of all group members. Almost all of them agree with the goal and want to make their meetings more active.

- ▪ *Hunt for the "No" and/or the alternative views by identifying weak signals and/or areas of disagreement:*

Some group members tend to be reluctant to share their views. A strong sign of false harmony is the absence of different views. The leader's task in that situation is to hunt for the "No" and/or areas of disagreement, even if that means detecting and amplifying weak signals of what may be alternative views.

> ➤ However, one group member is located in South Korea. In an informal break during the discussion, the leader encourages her to talk about her opinion. Her need in regard to improving meeting interaction differs from her colleagues' needs, all of whom are located in Europe. Because of the time difference, she has to join the bi-weekly meetings from her home at 11pm. Moreover, she can't access the meeting technology at home and wouldn't be able to join the video conferences. She symbolises the "No", in this case a weak and silent signal.

- ▪ *Spread the "No" and/or the alternative view and/or the weak signal and add minority wisdom:*

It is the leader's task to discuss the "No" (the area of disagreement or the alternative view) with all group members. Rather than thinking about how to get rid of the "No", the point is that all members discuss the differing opinion to find a solution that works for all. Equal weight and importance is given to the view that differs from the majority and its value and wisdom are discovered and appreciated. Many conflicts can be resolved at this point because, by considering and appreciating the other's perspective, positions, or interests, the lines of conflict are transformed into consensus, thereby enabling win–win situations. Typical questions in this context could be: What would help you, or what should be further improved or further implemented, to enable you to say "Yes" to the choice made by the majority of the group so far? How could the others include these new ideas into the already existing proposition?

> ➤ The other group members discuss their colleague's "No". They ask: "Why does she have to log on from home so late at night? We are a team and should all be equals. Isn't there an alternative?" By discussing the situation, they find and decide to implement a rotational model. The bi-weekly meetings are now held at different

times of day so that the Korean colleague is only working after hours from home every third week.

- *Say sorry and/or ask "What do you need?":*

If the "No" can't be integrated after all, it's important for the leader to show empathy and apologize to the minority member(s). She will ask the affected person(s) what the group can do instead to meet their needs? This may simply be a commitment to re-discuss the issue in question after a period of time.

➢ While the Korean group member is no longer required to join the bi-weekly meeting from home every time, she still needs to sacrifice one late evening every third week. The manager will now find out what the group can do for the colleague in Seoul to make the late-night session more comfortable for her. This could include asking her manager to allow her to come in a bit later on the mornings after the night meetings.

5. ***Plan in advance: How would you keep the topic(s) alive?***

Sustainable improvement requires behavioural change, which takes time and continuous practice and monitoring. It is therefore essential that the topics in question be included in a group's everyday work process. The critical topics should also be a constant on a group's meeting agendas. It is the leader's task to assess regularly how the group is doing in the improvement process.

➢ After each bi-weekly meeting, the group discusses how the rotation model is working for them and how meeting quality is developing.

6. ***Use indicators transparently: How would you monitor the topic(s)?***

Monitoring the improvement process is another crucial leadership task. The leader needs to control the process and adjust it as needed.

➢ After three months, the manager will conduct a more formal evaluation of the rotation model based on the regular discussions mentioned in Step 5.

A leadership behaviour that is necessary during negotiation processes, but often not explicitly mentioned, lies in applying the necessary degree of firmness to implementing what has been agreed upon. Exceptions from those standards should only be allowed when all group members agree. Equality is key to Deep Democracy and must be guarded even if that means investing much time and energy. Otherwise, people will do as they please causing chaos – which in virtuality can have even more serious ramifications than in face-to-face settings.

The following example shows how a global group within eBay is implementing the six steps of negotiating in critical-incidents sessions (see Chapter Nine for a comprehensive case study of that group). The group is located in the UK and in the USA. As part of a Virtual Performance Improvement process, they implemented a series of critical-incidents sessions, which helped them to increase Virtual Closeness and shape the Purple Space.

> ➢ Each session was prepared and led by a different group member who presented a critical incident from the global group's work, which was then discussed among the participants. Every session followed the six steps of negotiating. Participants came from both the US and the UK group; and in the case of the latter, from different locations across Europe. Eight different group members and two external moderators participated in every session. The sessions were structured voicing exercises. Discussing critical incidents, the participants practised voicing, giving and receiving feedback, and finding solutions for the respective issue together. In so doing, the group developed a culture of Shared Leadership.

When negotiating new, shared norms, behaviours, or tools it is important to remember that these don't replace the corresponding local norms. Rather, they exist in addition to the latter and complement them when colleagues are working together virtually. You can think of it in terms of backpacker cultures: members are familiar with both cultures (local and global/purple) and draw on either one as appropriate in the respective situation.

Textbox 7.2: Guidelines for Mediating Virtual Leadership

Clarity in Communication

- Do I understand truly and fully what I need to do in order to be successful in the project?
- Am I communicating my vision clearly and firmly enough? Am I sure that everybody has understood my message?
- Am I making optimal use of the existing communication channels in our day-to-day processes?
- Am I able to interpret, respect and appreciate the communication styles of the others?
- Am I contributing to the establishment of a feedback culture?

Cultural Sensitivity

- Am I open to cultural learning? Do I appreciate the cultural differences in values and styles within my working group and do I see diversity as a chance for further development of the group?
- Am I taking measures to support the sharing of cultural values and communication styles between project members and use them as levers for the project's success?
- Am I applying "face preserving" or "honour preserving" language?

Context Sensitivity

- Do I understand the context wherein my project colleagues live and work?
- Do I know their personal interests?
- Do I have a good understanding of how the individual project members think or feel when they work alone or in groups?
- Do all project members share the same perspective and, if not, what can I do in order to promote a shared perspective?

Boundary Crossing Activities

- Am I providing the right technological framework to advance goal-oriented formal and informal communication and cooperation between all parties involved?
- Am I providing the right mixture of media – face-to-face meetings, telephone and video conferencing, chat rooms, etc. – in order to conserve and boost relationships?
- Am I providing measures to nurture relationships between project members from different locations, organizations and job disciplines?
- Am I establishing rules, which allow project members to share workload if time zones, travelling activities and other challenges create significant hurdles to deliver results?
- Am I advancing the development of relations between my working group and other people or organizations critical for project success?

External Representation of Group

- Am I representing the interests of my working group effectively in meetings with top management or other decision-makers?
- Am I ensuring that the project group members are appreciated and rewarded for their performance?
- Am I ensuring adequate remuneration of the working group?

Shared Leadership

- Am I communicating clearly that all group members can take a leading role if this is compatible with the local culture?
- Am I nurturing self-organization within the work group?
- Are group members recognized for their valuable contributions or for their position/status?
- Am I able to let go or delegate when necessary (i.e. can I take on the role of a facilitator or coach?) and resume my leadership role if needed?
- Have I identified the appropriate project members for the various leadership roles in the different project steps?

Leadership intentions

- Am I sufficiently communicating project-related goals, schedules and organizational context to my local representatives?
- Have my representatives enough opportunity to participate so that they feel that their interests are being adequately represented?
- Have I reached a shared agreement about the process in order to ensure the accomplishment of project-related and personal goals?

Based on the concept of Ambassadorial Leadership and the corresponding checklist in Lojeski and Reilly (2008)

7.5 Leadership Presence: Availability and Visibility of the Virtual Leader

You will recall from Chapter Six that someone's Online Identity is essential to making him or her visible as a human being in virtual collaboration. A person's Online Identity is shaped by three types of virtual presence: social presence, leadership presence, and cognitive presence.

So far we have emphasized the concept of Online Identity and how leaders can provide a framework wherein group members are enabled to demonstrate social and cognitive presence (through structures, process design, technology, and facilitation). In this section, we will now focus on other important aspects of leadership presence.

In the often intangible world of virtual collaboration, one of the main challenges is to be and remain visible as a person. Leaders are usually very good at building relationships and guiding employees in face-to-face settings but often don't actually know how to make even themselves visible and available online (see Chapter Six for more information on availability) and to show leadership presence. Once they are introduced to the concept of Online Identity and the relevant medial and technological know how (Chapter Eight), this challenge vanishes in most cases.

Recommendations for Virtual Leaders

Availability also requires visibility. If group members don't know that their leader or manager is available online, the purpose is defeated.

Showing leadership presence online – making oneself visible – becomes easier when informal communication channels are made available in addition to formal ones. Sometimes these informal communication channels allow the user to be visible online (the green "Online" button on Skype, for example). When the leader regularly chooses not to be visibly available online he is similar to a leader who doesn't come to the office.

A leader can decide to have availability times. Once a week, for example, he could be on a web or telephone conference – WebEx or Skype, for example – or a chat during fixed office hours. Every group member can reach him and "talk" (chat) to him. If nobody shows up during the online office hours, that is ok, too. It is about clearly signalling presence and availability. A leader could also increase her presence by writing a blog to share her thoughts and ideas with all group members. This is also another great way to reduce email. Blog content must be interesting to group members, though.

These strategies are "pull" strategies that are based on the Self-Organization Skills of group members. The same strategy should be pursued in regular meetings (on a daily or weekly basis). By asking "How" questions (instead of "Why" questions and/or giving commands) and having a coaching/mentoring attitude, the virtual leader shows visibility and leadership presence. This, in turn, allows group members to feel that the leader really cares about them and their contributions to the group. This especially helps in situations where Self-Organization Skills are not yet well developed and where the local culture is strongly power-oriented.

Increased visibility in the virtual world requires the leader to build a professional Online Identity. For a leader, having a continuous leadership presence is clearly of particular importance.

A leader's Online Identity must be especially visible. In order to build it, he should be aware of how he is perceived in face-to-face settings and consider how to transport this perception into the virtual setting. He needs to ask: "Who am I and how can I show myself to my colleagues via media? How do I build and maintain relationships over the distance? What can I do with media that I cannot do face-to-face?"

The following example demonstrates this point. Most social media or community platforms offer dynamic user profiles. If a user likes the contribution of another user (for example, in a discussion forum), he can go to that person's profile and find out what he or she has written in other contexts and what kind of cues that user has left on other media platforms. This will give him a more holistic picture of the person. A leader can capitalize on that knowledge by professionalizing his Online Identity, thereby exerting increased leadership influence in his environment.

The ability of leaders to influence processes and people (instead of pushing them) will be of increasing importance in the future. A good example of this is Barack Obama's online presidential election campaign. Through being available and visible online, leadership presence forms the necessary basis for influencing.

7.6 Managing the Links

The links that virtual groups use in their work are the media available to them. It is through media that members link up with each other, including their leader. Being able to manage those links is therefore an essential skill of the virtual leader, so much so that we dedicated Chapter Eight to the topic (and see also Chapter Six on E-Culture).

In their seminal work on virtual teams, Lipnack and Stamps argue that leaders in non-virtual organizations focus on leading people and their purpose of working together. They added a third dimension for virtual leadership: managing the links that allow virtual groups to operate[9]. Virtual leaders need to manage the links that help people connect with each other and the links that help people connect with the purposes of their work. As a consequence, the media should match the purpose (project spaces versus community spaces, for example) and the media and their features should be compatible with the personal preferences and the local cultural contexts. These links are the media and technology used in virtual collaboration, at which we take a detailed look in Chapter Eight.

Recommendations for Virtual Leaders

✓ Select links that work for your group and its purpose. It is your task either to negotiate which media your group will use (also based on individual preferences) or, when the collaboration period is rather short and there isn't enough time to negotiate links, to make a decision about which media to use. You then need to enable the group to build the competences required to use those media, implement them rigorously, and make sure to keep them active.

✓ Rather than using too many media, agree on a few and use them very actively. People will use formal and informal communication channels only when they are filled with life. As a rule, there should always be at least one formal and one informal channel as well as one synchronous and one asynchronous media available and employed that are not email or phone.

✓ As a virtual leader, you need to use those links, too! By role modelling how to build an Online Identity and being available through the links, you make their use attractive for the other group members. As a leader, you also need to monitor and correct media use in a supportive fashion.

Notes

1 See, for example, Ghislaine Caulat (2012) *Virtual Leadership: Learning to lead differently*, Libri; Lojeski, Karen Sobel (2009) *Leading the Virtual Workforce: How Great Leaders Transform Organizations in the 21ˢᵗ Century*; Jaclyn Kostner (1996) *Virtual Leadership*.

2 See Kotter (2001) for the difference between management skills and leadership skills. He argues that management is about coping with complexity whereas leadership is about coping with rapid change.

3 http://www.pateauconsultants.com/en/index.php.

4 Ulrich (2005) – In Susanne Ulrich's model, which we have adopted, "fake tolerance" is called "apparent tolerance".

5 Stefan Meister and Marcus Hildebrandt are working on an evidence-based diagnostic instrument for assessing feedback preferences, the InterPersonal Feedback Profiler.

6 http://www.deepdemocracyinstitute.org/deep-democracy-explained.html. Unlike "classical" democracy, which focuses on majority rule, Deep Democracy suggests that all voices, states of awareness, and frameworks of reality are important. Deep Democracy also suggests that all the information carried within these voices, levels of awareness, and frameworks is needed to understand the complete process of a system. Deep Democracy is an attitude that focuses on the awareness of voices that are both central and marginal. This type of awareness can be focused on groups, organizations, one's own inner experiences, people in conflict, and so on. Allowing oneself to take seriously seemingly unimportant events and feelings can often bring unexpected solutions to both group and inner conflicts. Although the term and the concept of Deep Democracy are now used by various groups in different ways, Mindell formulates their common denominator: Deep Democracy is the experience of a process of flow in which all actors on the stage are needed to create the play that is being watched.

7 Schütze und Hildebrandt (2006).

8 Lewis, Myrna: Inside the No, http://www.deep-democracy.net.

9 Lipnack and Stamps (2000).

CHAPTER EIGHT

Media and Technology

8.1 Using the Right Media for the Right Purpose

8.2 The Heartbeat of Virtual Groups, Teams, and Networks

8.3 Different Levels of Maturity in Virtual Communication

8.4 Media Mix

Technology provides the tools to interact with one another on a global scale. While asynchronous communication (writing letters) has existed for thousands of years, contemporary communication is increasingly characterized by synchronous interactions. In our globalized world, people have to increasingly align their calendars to enable joint phone or videoconferences. In this chapter, we examine media use in different virtual group contexts and suggest a particular mix of synchronous and asynchronous communication streams.

8.1 Using the Right Media for the Right Purpose

Every communication tool has strengths and weaknesses that vary according to the situation and to user preferences or cultural context. While a medium's strengths are therefore not absolute but always relative, media can be classified in three terms:

- Information richness;

- The number of people that can interact simultaneously (1:1 or 1:n or n:m)[1];

- The time it takes to get a reaction to a contribution: synchronous (interaction partners interact in real time, for example in a chat) or asynchronous communication (reactions are significantly delayed, for example through email).

Synchronous and Asynchronous Media

Marginalizing asynchronous tools such as blogs, wikis, or discussion forums, many organizations follow a constant trend towards more synchronous tools including VOIP (e.g. Skype), SMS, micro blogging (e.g. Twitter), or email on mobile phones. Communication processes are increasingly accelerated by the fast-growing use of synchronous media. This is complemented by a growth in the use of more integrated communication systems. It has become good practice to run a chat parallel to a telephone conference in order to record meeting minutes instantly (a great support for non-native English speakers or groups facing language issues). Likewise, application sharing during video conferences has been established as an effective tool to focus on documents discussed online.

In light of these trends, it is crucial that virtual leaders create a tool portfolio for the virtual collaboration of their groups even if this is found to be difficult (which it often is). Ideally, this media framework is negotiated among all group members and answers the following questions:

- Which media exist and are available to every group member?

- Why do group members use specific media and particular features of these (identification of existing competences and good practice)?

- Which media could be used for which purpose?

The second question addresses personal and cultural preferences and experiences and therefore doesn't lend itself to generalization. There is, however, much tested wisdom on choosing the "right" media for the "right" purposes, which we will look at now.

Divergent and Convergent Communication Processes

Most communication processes can be categorized as divergent or convergent. In divergent processes, the communicator seeks out the different existing opinions, ideas, and perspectives on dealing with a given context, thereby increasing the amount of relevant information as much as possible. In convergent communication, on the other hand, the objective is to reach a point of conclusion, to come to a decision, to summarize, or to solve a conflict. The amount of relevant information is decreased as far as possible.

Figure 8.1: Divergent and Convergent Communication Processes

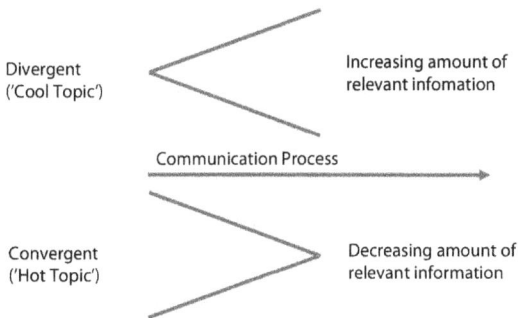

Divergent
('Cool Topic')

Increasing amount of
relevant infomation

Communication Process

Convergent
('Hot Topic')

Decreasing amount of
relevant information

The more time people have to think about options, new ideas, and solutions to challenges, the higher the quality and quantity of collected information will be. On the other hand, if people want to make a decision (when all options are on the table and clear to everyone and the decision makers are on board and involved) this is best done synchronously. The reason is that in synchronous communication, others' immediate reactions can be perceived and reacted to accordingly, thereby speeding up the decision-making process. These observations lead to a rule of thumb[2] about the match of communication processes and media.

- Asynchronous media are great for divergent communication processes.
- Synchronous media are great for convergent communication processes.

A typical example of divergent communication is brainstorming. The quality of the results of a brainstorming process is increased if participants have sufficient time to think about their own ideas as well as the others' contributions. By being able to brainstorm for about a week using asynchronous media like a discussion forum, a blog, or a wiki, a group is very likely to come up with better results than during an hour of face-to-face idea production.

This is especially true when cultural aspects are of concern. In some cultures, people are reluctant to come up with ideas in face-to-face encounters because they may feel exposed to the group and at risk of losing face. This is different in the virtual world. Asynchronous online brainstorming is therefore a culturally sensible solution in addition to promising better overall results. Another advantage of asynchronous text-based work is that it helps overcome language barriers more easily as people can take the time they need to translate and think about contributions. Finally, if a group environment allows posting contributions anonymously, the full potential of brainstorming can be realized.

Anonymity can also be useful in certain synchronous settings. Using electronic group decision-making or feedback instruments may increase the honesty and authenticity of feedback and decisions.

When employees are asked for input or feedback on a decision, results usually differ significantly depending on whether they are expected to voice their opinions in front of colleagues and managers or allowed to present their views anonymously in a virtual space.

While the asynchronous world is the realm of creative and divergent processes, synchronous communication is best suited for soliciting immediate responses, including non-verbal reactions. This allows refining the outcomes of a communication process step by step in real time, but at the cost of reducing the degree of freedom for coming up with a better solution, decision, or joint statement or summary.

Figure 8.2: Synchronous and Asynchronous Media in Convergent and Divergent Communication Processes

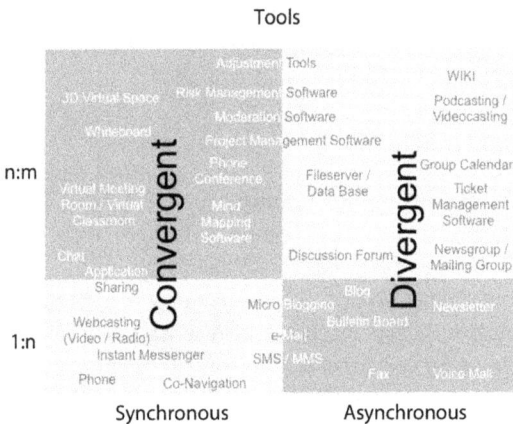

The two tables below contain suggestions on how to use different media in different communication situations.

Table 8.1: Purpose, Media, and Synchronicity

Communication Situation	Media	Synchronous / Asynchronous
Getting to know each other	F2F, Chat, Forum	Both
Asking questions	F2F, Telephone, Email, Chat, IM, Forum	Both
Solving conflict	F2F	Synchronous
Negotiating	F2F, Telephone, Video conference, Telephone conference	Synchronous
Exchanging confidential information	F2F, (IM, SMS), Telephone	Synchronous
Taking decisions	F2F, Chat, Video conference, Telephone conference	Synchronous
Brainstorming	Forum, F2F Tool	Both
Informing	Email, WIKI	Push or Pull Strategy
Keeping in contact	Telephone, Email, Chat, IM, SMS	Both
Distributing information quickly	Telephone, Video conference, IM, SMS	Synchronous

Table 8.2: Media and Purpose

Media	Communication Situation
F2F	Getting to know each other / Solving conflicts / Negotiating / Exchanging information / Making decisions
Email	Informing / Asking questions / Keeping in contact
Telephone	Asking Questions / Keeping in contact / Quickly distributing information / Exchanging confidential information
Telephone conference, Video conference	Getting to know each other / Negotiating / Making decisions / Quickly distributing information
Chat	Keeping in contact / Getting to know each other / Asking questions
Forum	Asking questions / Getting to know each other / Brainstorming
WIKI	Informing / Getting to know each other / Asking questions
IM	Keeping in contact / Asking questions / Quickly distributing information
SMS	Keeping in contact / Asking questions / Quickly distributing information

Formal and Informal Communication Processes

Communication processes can be further classified as formal or informal. Certain media like instant messaging are better suited for informal communication than others. Providing and managing formal as well as informal interaction spaces is an important success factor for leading groups in a virtual and intercultural context to high performance.

In collective cultures, for example, it is important for virtual participants to consult regularly within the home group before and after a decision, and during a brainstorming session or on-going discussion to ensure social norms such as hierarchies are respected. It is therefore necessary (and good practice) to allow for informal breaks during virtual meetings or for instant messaging or chatting processes to take place simultaneously. While this particularly applies to participants from collective cultures, it could be good practice in any event. After all, people from more individualistic cultures are often also under certain hierarchical restrictions, which force them to check in with their home fronts on a regular basis.

Figure 8.3: Interaction Spaces: Examples

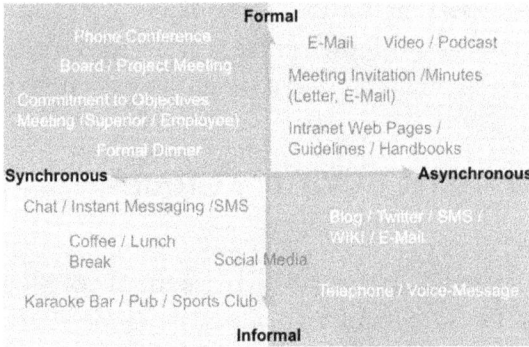

Formal

Phone Conference
Board / Project Meeting
Commitment to Objectives
Meeting (Superior / Employee)
Formal Dinner

E-Mail   Video / Podcast

Meeting Invitation /Minutes
(Letter, E-Mail)

Intranet Web Pages /
Guidelines / Handbooks

Synchronous   **Asynchronous**

Chat / Instant Messaging /SMS

Coffee / Lunch
Break   Social Media

Karaoke Bar / Pub / Sports Club

Blog / Twitter / SMS /
WIKI / E-Mail

Telephone / Voice-Message

Informal

Virtual Group Kick Off

This media-usage knowledge suggests an innovative perspective on the traditional approach of starting a new group with a face-to-face kick-off meeting. Understanding that face-to-face time is best suited for solving problems, conflicts and taking decisions, it actually makes more sense to start a virtual team virtually, especially when chances for an all-group face-to-face meeting within the first few months or even the first year are small.

Orchestrating a virtual kick off requires leaders to design a set of asynchronous and synchronous media interventions to help people get to know each other, create a shared understanding of group goals, and launch the first joint tasks. Using discussion forums, wikis, blogs, or web conferencing can lead to a very successful virtual kick off.

The kick-off phase often has a honeymoon quality, given all the initial communication. In such comprehensive dialogue, critical conflicts tend to appear less. Problems usually start when a group settles into remote collaboration and the real issues and diverging interpretations of the seemingly "shared rules and mental models" become transparent. In circumstances of restricted opportunities for face-to-face meetings, these are better saved for resolving such conflicts. "Wasting" the face-to-face joker on the kick off could lead to veritable disasters because serious conflict is hardly resolved successfully online. We therefore recommend postponing the first face-to-face meeting until a group have worked together for a certain period of time, ideally about three to six months (depending on the development speed of the group). Face-to-face interaction will then prove very useful to revisit any decisions made so far and take a closer look at the virtual performance.

8.2 The Heartbeat of Virtual Groups, Teams, and Networks

Time spent in shared dialogue will increase the Work Schedule Overlaps necessary for successful virtual collaboration. But how much overlap is required? How much time should be spent in shared dialogue and how frequently or regularly should such dialogues occur?

According to Martha Maznevski and Katherine Chudoba[3], the synchronous activities of virtual groups create a particular rhythm – a heartbeat. A healthy heartbeat is created through the combination of regular face-to-face and synchronous virtual meetings using the full potential of available media. The balance of frequent, regular contact in both worlds pumps oxygen and blood into the life of the group. The rhythm is what "drives... time to build and develop a deep level of understanding of each other's background and knowledge"[4]. The first image below contains the "recording" of an effective virtual team's heartbeat, nicely showing how it differs from that of an ineffective virtual group, as seen in the second image below.

The development speed of a team – the time it needs to make decisions, solve problems, and resolve conflicts – is defined by the rhythm of its synchronous meetings. If this rhythm is regular, meaningful communication rituals can be introduced to increase member cohesion and participation, in turn leading to higher performance. And of course, regularity allows group members to come to meetings well prepared as opposed to being stressed out by irregular or surprise events.

It is important to understand that face-to-face meetings do not need to coincide with major decision making. In fact, Maznevski found that "the most effective virtual teams do not necessarily use face-to-face time for... major communication issues"[5].

Figure 8.4: Regular Heartbeat of a Virtual Group

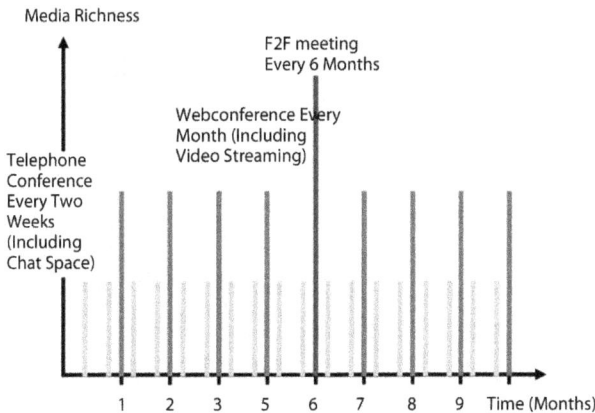

Media Richness

F2F meeting
Every 6 Months

Webconference Every
Month (Including
Video Streaming)

Telephone
Conference
Every Two
Weeks
(Including
Chat Space)

1   2   3   5   6   7   8   9   Time (Months)

Adapted with permission from Maznevski, M., and Chudoba, K.M. (2000) Bridging space over time: Global virtual team dynamics and effectiveness. *Organization Science* 11(5): 473–92, Copyright 2000, the Institute for Operations Research and the Management Sciences, 5521 Research Park Drive, Suite 200, Catonsville, MD 21228.

The above image depicts an example of a regular heartbeat. The peaks indicate the level of information richness, with face-to-face interaction reaching the highest level and video or telephone conferences rising not quite as high.

Figure 8.5: Irregular Heartbeat of a Virtual Group

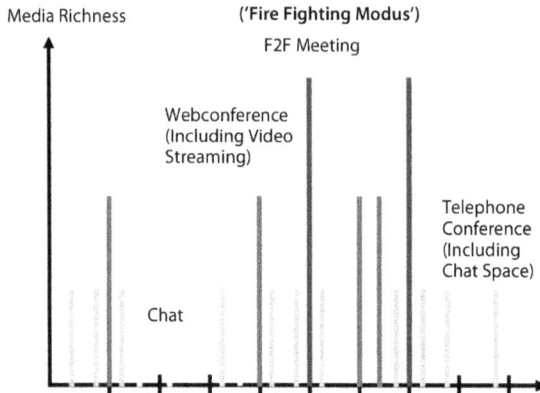

Adapted with permission from Maznevski, M., and Chudoba, K.M. (2000) Bridging space over time: Global virtual team dynamics and effectiveness. *Organization Science* 11(5): 473–92, Copyright 2000, the Institute for Operations Research and the Management Sciences, 5521 Research Park Drive, Suite 200, Catonsville, MD 21228.

The amount of time that passes between face-to-face heartbeats depends on a group's tasks, specifically their complexity and interdependence, as well as on the quality of group-member cohesion.

Some virtual groups never meet face-to-face at all. Even more than in groups that share face-to-face time, the regularity of their heartbeat will be shaped by how they use available media for specific purposes.

When a group has too-frequent synchronous meetings, its asynchronous communication tends to break down. During the week before a face-to-face meeting, people tend to think that most communication can be postponed until then.

An optimal mix and rhythm for the use of asynchronous and synchronous media therefore exists for every group. The challenge is to find and establish it.

The virtual leader's role in this is that of the pacemaker who sets the rhythm. Groups tend to connect only when things get difficult but they really need to have a healthy heartbeat to stay fit in the long run. The responsibility for watching the group's health rests with the leader.

8.3 Different Levels of Maturity in Virtual Communication

Different levels of virtualization of communication and cooperation emerge when examining existing virtual groups, teams, or networks.

The choice of specific electronic collaboration tools in a group usually depends on:

- Their availability for every group member,

- The degree to which group members master the different tools, and

- Members' personal media preferences, which are partly influenced by their national culture.

These three factors determine the different existing levels of maturity of virtualization in organizations. We have seen that efficient virtual collaboration relies on tools for synchronous and asynchronous, as well as formal and informal, communication and cooperation spaces. The level of virtual maturity in a group increases according to the quality of the features of these tools, the extent to which they are integrated, and the degree of digitalization of human communication channels.

The following five levels describe an ideal trajectory of growing maturity in virtual communication, visualized in the image below.

Level 1: Email and telephone
The majority of virtual groups, even in high-tech organizations, use email and phone as their main channels for global communication. While most groups also have access to video-conference technology, this is used much less due to its technical

inflexibility. Video-conference rooms require advance booking; they may not be available in all locations of the organization; and the physical presence of all members in the room is necessary, which is often not feasible due to individual schedules, particularly outside of core office hours. Email and telephone, on the contrary, allow greater flexibility and spontaneity.

Level 2: Shared data space
A higher level of maturity is reached when groups, in addition to email and telephone, have access to a shared online space in which all members can store, retrieve, and exchange data.

Level 3: Variety of synchronous and asynchronous tools
The next maturity level is based on an increased variety of either synchronous or asynchronous tools or both, commonly used by all group members. Asynchronous tools usually include a WIKI, a discussion forum, or a blog. Chat or instant-messaging functions are often added for synchronous communication.

Figure 8.6: Maturity Levels of Virtualization

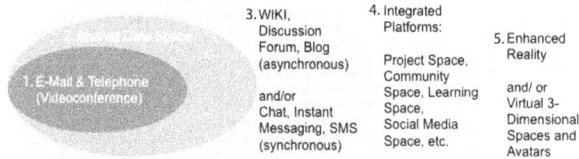

3. WIKI, Discussion Forum, Blog (asynchronous) and/or Chat, Instant Messaging, SMS (synchronous)

4. Integrated Platforms: Project Space, Community Space, Learning Space, Social Media Space, etc.

5. Enhanced Reality and/ or Virtual 3-Dimensional Spaces and Avatars

1. E-Mail & Telephone (Videoconference)

Level 4: Integration
Maturity further grows once the above elements (email, telephone, shared data spaces, and other synchronous and asynchronous tools) are integrated into one technological platform that is optimized with respect to a certain purpose of virtual collaboration. This could be virtual team spaces, project-management spaces, community spaces, web conference spaces, learning spaces, and such like. When entering these spaces, users are updated on the

activities that have occurred there since their last visit. Moreover, because voice is usually transmitted digitally (VOIP), using such spaces offers new possibilities of merging media.

Level 5: Three-dimensional virtual spaces or enhanced reality
This is the future of virtual group work, pioneered already by a number of global organizations. In 3D virtual spaces, group members meet as avatars and often feel as if they were physically together in the same room in spite of the actual geographical distance between them. Such platforms feature inbuilt social media and other tools needed for effective collaboration. A flip chart, for example, looks like a flip chart but is technically a white board with underlying application sharing.

With enhanced reality and three-dimensionality being introduced into virtual collaboration, we are certain that new categories and dimensions of Virtual Closeness will emerge. The experience of being immersed in virtual space is likely to generate fresh aspects of virtual group work. Moreover, we can already see first examples of a sixth level of virtualization related to implanting digital media into human bodies, which will drastically change the way we work and communicate. We will leave the consequences of such development for Virtual Closeness to future publications.

Back in our current, immediate reality, we face the general challenge of encountering a heterogeneous mix of media availability, Media Competences, and media preferences within virtual groups. For virtually mature group members, giving up their favourite media in order to accommodate colleagues on a lower level of maturity might feel like going back to a digital stone age. Conversely, less tech-savvy members may experience fear or worry about not being able to handle new media. Here, generational gaps often become particularly visible.

How can groups best deal with these gaps in virtual experience? We recommend that groups not go for the lowest common denominator of virtual maturity among their members. Instead, they should try to reach the highest maturity level with the least complexity that leads to the highest possible level of performance in their specific context, thereby creating a purple interaction space. Taking the human factor into account is crucial for this. Both sides – the tech-savvy members and the less tech-savvy ones – have to enter into a type of learning partnership that supports the latter in catching up, similar to overcoming language issues. A good start is agreeing to introduce a more advanced tool that can be used on different levels according to individual Media Competence. While some members may quickly exhaust the functionality of the tool, others begin by practising the basic functions. As in every group learning process, this is about accepting shared responsibility to help the newcomers reach a higher level, even at the price of temporarily working with a tool that might not be on the highest level.

Finally, when creating Virtual Closeness in groups with individuals on different maturity levels of virtualization (and thus the software of the Purple Space), the more virtually mature members also need to have high maturity levels in Media Competence, Feedback Competence, Communication Styles, and Global Netiquette Skills. Those with lower maturity levels have to be trained and supported to grow in these areas.

8.4 Media Mix

In order to establish a communication routine that allows all group members to participate according to their cultural and individual preferences, virtual leaders must aim to create a high level of member involvement and activity in the available media tools. The failure to exploit available media channels fully will not only amplify any cultural challenges but also fail to empower members to participate in the group's work and identify with it.

The extent of member participation in media communication significantly depends on the different possibilities people can choose for interaction. Three of our human senses pave the way to optimal interaction in virtuality: seeing, hearing, and partially also feeling (i.e. speaking with your fingers on the keyboard or with your mouth into a receiver); while taste and smell are not yet directly engaged. Being able simultaneously to see colleagues (or materials), hear them, and interact with them, either through writing or talking or both, will immediately trigger people's motivation to really use virtual links to communicate and cooperate. As in physical interaction, the more senses one can activate to relate to someone or something emotionally, the more one is pulled into the process of relating and encouraged to act. However, those of you who have experienced dining in the dark will appreciate that muting one sense (sight) can enhance tasting and smelling. The same applies to media, in that it can be useful to focus on less rich media.

As with the different learning types, the details of individual combination preferences may vary. Different people learn best with differing mixes of visual, audible, or haptic elements. But offering an option for combining multiple learning techniques is a basic essential. Hence leaders should aim to include the three levels of seeing, hearing, and the kinesthetic sense into all media use.

Of course, effective media use presupposes adequate skills and competences in facilitating virtual processes. All group members, including managers, need to be comfortable navigating different media. This is not always easy and requires continuous practice. The following examples from our work with virtual groups portray typical challenges in media use and offer solutions to overcome them based on combining different media tools.

> ➤ *Conference call: No questions asked, no comments given?*
> Just like in physical meetings, not everybody joining a conference call is motivated or comfortable to participate actively. Often, it is the same handful of people who do the talking. Moreover, meeting minutes often summarize the contents of conference calls sufficiently for people to rely on them and skip the actual call, either physically or through mental absence. A good way to tackle this issue is to control the commitment and decision levels attached to the call by combining video, voice, and chat with a shared screen part. If one group member protocols whatever is agreed upon on a shared screen seen by everyone, the meeting contents take on a higher level of importance because participants can hear and see them at the same time.

In an international group, it is useful to ask a native speaker to take over the task of written documentation. Non-native speakers often experience difficulties understanding natives due to their faster speech or use of slang. If native speakers do the writing, not only do they slow down and become easier to understand, but others may feel more comfortable contributing without worrying too much about not saying the right thing in the right way. Participation is further encouraged when questions and comments can be placed both verbally and in writing, using a white board or a chat or a shared document. While many people are afraid of speaking English, they often feel more confident writing in English. Similarly, it is considered impolite in some cultures to ask questions during a presentation, thus keeping involvement low; while in other cultures it is normal to interrupt the speakers at any time, thereby rupturing the presentation flow. If members can place their questions and ideas in a chat running parallel to the verbal conversations, the amount of comments and virtual activity will increase noticeably while interruptions will decrease. Motivation to participate will increase significantly.

To enhance this further, leaders or other group members with a good command of the common language might ask questions regarding challenging vocabulary, technical terms or abbreviations, even though they know the answer or can guess what it might be. Someone then has the task of putting the explanations in a glossary tool (using a wiki, blog, discussion forum, or data base). In this way, they encourage others with a lesser command of the shared language also to ask for clarification when needed, thus creating an internal culture of openness, taking care of each other, and building a shared knowledge base.

If language issues are a very strong challenge, it is crucial to distribute written documentation of key issues before the call and to take frequent breaks. These should be used to allow those with a lesser command of the language to generate questions using an application sharing tool that allows different people to write in the same document. If a "face loss" is to be feared, these questions could even be submitted anonymously.

From a cultural point of view, it can sometimes be advisable to set up culturally homogenous groups that discuss agenda topics in parallel virtual break-out rooms (multiple chats, parallel phone conferences, etc.). A speaker will then present the results to the large group.

> *Virtual meeting: Who, why, what, and when?*
>
> Employing multiple media strategies as in the above example requires improving facilitation and introducing certain structures into meeting routines. We have often heard people say, "I wonder why I'm in this conference call at all." A good facilitator should clearly state why group members are supposed to participate in a virtual meeting and what is expected from them during the call. If these two things are not obvious to participants, they will likely consider a meeting to be a waste of time and revert to reading the minutes in the future. Increasing the degree of Shared Leadership when preparing the agenda can be a good solution. This can be done using a wiki, a discussion forum, or a shared document to jointly set up the meeting goals and the agenda and define the different roles and responsibilities of participants.

To improve meeting structure and increase the level of participation, we use the so-called team clock. In a call with more than five participants, using a team clock helps to structure members' airtime. Due to the clockwise rotation, they know exactly when they will be asked to speak. We recommend using the team clock three to five times during a session.

Figure 8.7: The Team Clock

➢ *Meeting purpose*

A group had regular Friday meetings dreaded by most members. Those meetings took four hours during which every participant reported for half an hour on developments in their respective locations, including information about customers, key accounts, and so forth. Nobody really listened to what was being said. When we asked the group leaders why they did not break once an hour for ten minutes, they revealed their fear of people not coming back to the meeting afterwards. We suggested that holding virtual meetings that way is the same as conducting a workshop without breaks because of the facilitator's fear of people leaving. This case portrays poor facilitation and planning skills. Having regular meetings for the sole purpose of sharing information is not useful. Pure information is best shared in writing and asynchronously; listening to it is not necessary. In (virtual) meetings, many people are attentive during the first five to ten minutes. If they have no chance to become involved until then, most start focusing on other matters like answering their emails.

The solution we created with this group rested on a profound change of the meeting setup. Meeting time was reduced to two hours. The initial information exchange was turned into gossip about the week's events in the different locations (social presence). And the actual information had to be sold: Everyone who had something to say was asked to write it down on a piece of paper. They then had slots of five minutes to sell their information to the others, arguing why this information is important and should be read. Opinions were exchanged the following week. Suddenly, it became interesting to participate in the Friday meetings, mainly because insider information normally confined to water-cooler and coffee-machine areas was shared and an informal atmosphere appropriate for a Friday was created.

➢ *Simulating reality*

A leader located in Europe manages a very successful virtual group spread around the globe that excels at using media to simulate reality. Specifically, he introduced a group chat function for private, internal exchange. In an office, we can easily approach a colleague next door to discuss ideas and ask for input – a crucial function of creativity. Obviously, this is not so easy in virtual groups. The manager therefore implemented chat rooms wherein group members could interact by asking questions and exchanging thoughts, thereby helping each other in real time. What made this model so successful, however, is that this group also uses the chat room for social interaction facilitated by the leader. When arriving at the office on Monday mornings, group members briefly enter the social chat room to greet colleagues and share a bit about their weekend – just what they would do if they were collocated in a single office.

These examples of mixing media in virtual cooperation show several things. First, establishing a routine of combining media for virtual communication is a continuous process of negotiating. Second, it is much more effective for virtual groups to have just a few links and really work hard to keep those alive (Shared Leadership and Self-Organization Skills), instead of scattering communication across too many different virtual spaces. Third, employing media well is a management skill and can be trained. A manager needs to decide which media to employ and then regularly remind his people to use them. If a group agrees to store documents only on SharePoint, for example, but one member repeatedly distributes documents in email, the manager needs to intervene and exercise control by communicating. Such leadership will create good practices and shared behaviours within the media channel. While providing and managing different media links is a leadership task, all virtual groups profit immensely if this task is adequately shared amongst members. The initial time invested into negotiating a virtual meeting culture will pay off greatly once routines are established.

Interestingly, Majchrzak et al. found that the media least popular with virtual groups for effective collaboration are email and video conferencing[6]. Email is prophesied to be on the decline more broadly[7], largely due to its impracticality arising from being made for one-to-one exchanges. In teams, especially in virtual ones, private email use between single colleagues can quickly lead to trust issues and feelings of being excluded. On the other hand, as most of us have probably experienced, copying every group member into every single email exchange quickly leads to flooded email accounts and, potentially, the habitual deleting of unread emails. Moreover, documents tend to get lost in email or confusion about the latest version arises. The main problems with video conferencing are seen in needing to be in a specific location to participate and having to put up with slow connections and frustrating time delays. Teleconferencing, on the other hand, is popular because it allows people the flexibility to join from their homes, even later in the evening or very early in the morning.

Notes

1　Media are classified according to the number of people who can use them simultaneously and whether they are interactive or not: 1:1 – only two people can communicate with each other (instant messaging point to point); 1:n – one person can send a message to n others (video streaming); n:m – all users can be in contact with each other and everyone can see their communication (chat).

2　When presenting this rule to our customer, Colin Main, he came up with another great rule of thumb: emotional topics –> synchronous media; cool/factual topics –> asynchronous media.

3　Maznevski and Chudoba (2000).

4　Ibid.

5　Maznevski et al (2006).

6　Majchrzak et al. (2004).

7　Atos Origin intends to eliminate internal email by 2014, http://boydio.wordpress.com/2011/03/08/no-more-email-in-3-years-good-luck-with-that/.

•••

CHAPTER NINE

The Virtual Performance Assessment Tool (VPA) and the Virtual Performance Improvement Process (VPI)

9.1   The Virtual Performance Assessment Tool (VPA)

9.2   The Virtual Performance Improvement Process (VPI)

The Virtual Performance Improvement is a structured and on-going process to optimize the performance of a virtual group. Before we look more closely at the VPI process and a number of case studies that show how such a process can be designed, we would like to point out some procedural aspects of the Virtual Performance Assessment (VPA) tool, which is an integrated part of the VPI process.

9.1 The Virtual Performance Assessment Tool (VPA)

In order to help groups to create and foster Virtual Closeness and reduce complexity in Purple Spaces, we have developed the Virtual Performance Assessment (VPA) tool and the Virtual Performance Improvement (VPI) process. VPA is a diagnostic tool that measures the twenty dimensions introduced above in the context of a virtual team, group, or network. VPA is an integrated and integral (but not the only) element of a VPI process. It provides the basic data upon which the individual performance-improvement process is modelled. It is a pragmatic approach to building the Purple Space and Virtual Closeness. Conducting the VPA helps virtual groups to understand where their potential for improvement lies. It helps leaders and consultants to design a sound process of virtual-group set up in the initial phase.

VPA: The Diagnostic Tool

The Virtual Performance Assessment is an online questionnaire based on the five categories and 20 dimensions for creating Virtual Closeness introduced in the previous chapters. Every dimension is covered by two questions (40 questions in total) concerning different levels of maturity or different aspects of Virtual Closeness.

The questionnaire is completed by all group members including leaders. Each member gets individual access to the group survey. Once the questionnaire has been completed by single members or the entire group, reports can be generated in several ways showing:

- Individual members' results

- Accumulated group results

- Accumulated sub-group results (In a global group with a German and a British sub-group, for example, their results can be evaluated separately as well as cumulatively.)

- Differing perceptions (marked with graphic elements), for example between the group and the leader.

The results are converted into a graphic output. The different evaluation options allow the user to discern differing perspectives of participants and analyze whether these are individual or location-wide phenomena.

Exhibit 9.1: VPA Output Example

VPA measures the users' perception of Virtual Closeness concerning the status of their virtual collaboration processes, thus producing descriptive, non-judgmental results. Low scores do not indicate a negative result but point to the specific perception of one or all group members at a certain point of time.These results present a virtual group's "tune", its "melody" as perceived by the individual group members, at a given point in time. This tune can be based on a single melody shared by group members if their perceptions are similar; or it can be a portfolio, or at worst a cacophony, of melodies if perceptions vary.

The assessment thus creates a framework that shows potential "hot spots of Virtual Closeness" for a group's virtual collaboration and identifies specific starting points for interventions.

Application Scenarios for VPA

Developed from an Organization Development perspective and as a diagnostic tool, VPA fulfils multiple functions. Apart from being an assessment tool, it also encourages discussion and learning about the twenty dimensions of creating Virtual Closeness. For a virtual group, filling out a VPA and discussing the different perspectives and the corresponding experience encourages building or improving a common identity and the design of a new collaboration space that is best suited for this group or organization: its own customized Purple

Space. It is therefore simultaneously a first step towards creating Virtual Closeness and the initial building block of a Virtual Performance Improvement process, at the beginning of or at any point during a collaborative process.

VPA can be used in a variety of scenarios:

- In the context of a coaching process conducted by a leader in charge of a virtual group in an intercultural setting

- In the context of a group development process

- As a needs-analysis tool in the pre-phase of a training or workshop

- As a learning evaluation tool before and after the learning process in the context of learning interventions concerning virtual, intercultural cooperation and organization development

- As a benchmarking tool: one group's performance compared to other groups' results saved in the data base (available as soon as there are enough data)

- As an Organization Development instrument.

Textbox 9.1: Orientation Questions

Orientation Questions to Identify "Hot Spots" and Causal Connections within VPA Results

1. What are the highest and lowest scores in the different categories?
2. What could be the interpretation of the highest or lowest scores?
   -> Use coaching questions
3. Are these extreme scores connected to the strengths or potential areas of improvement of the group?
   Examples: A high score in "Time Shared in Dialogue" could be a strength in the sense that the group is using this precious time to solve problems. On the other hand, it could point out challenges: "Due to many conflicts and distrust, the group has to spend more time on synchronous meetings than the members can really cope with..."
4. Could there be a connection between the extreme scores within one category?
   Example: "Due to the fact that there is a high value in 'Geographic Advantage' there is also a low value in 'Work Schedule Overlap' as the group has to manage large time-zone separations..."
5. Could there be a causal connection between the extreme score in one category with the corresponding one in another? If yes, what could be the corresponding headline?
   Examples:
   - *"Because the group has little organizational relevance, the team members do not identify with the objectives of the group...", or*
   - *"Due to the high self-organization competence there is also a high score in shared leadership..." or*
   - *"Because there is little management attraction with respect to the group, it has a very high autonomy and is therefore strong in 'Shared Leadership' and 'Identification with the Group and its Objectives'..."*
6. Having identified the "hot spots" and the causal connections:
   - How could one use the strengths of the group to improve the weak points?
   - Are there levers due to causal connections: could the optimization of one weaker point lead also to improvements in other dimensions?

9.2 The Virtual Performance Improvement Process (VPI)

The Virtual Performance Improvement process is designed and implemented based on and within the framework that results from a VPA intervention. Following the principle of attractiveness, it builds on a group's strengths in order to improve any existing deficits. A VPI process can be started with a VPA to elicit the group's tune.

When supporting an organization in its efforts to improve virtual performance, different levels of entry exist:

- A mandate may cover working with separate teams, groups, or networks

- Or it may be for improving the quality of virtual collaboration within the organization on a higher level, requiring working with whole clusters of groups, teams, or networks.

Depending on the mandate, different approaches may be required contingent on the parameters of the specific context. Some aspects not available for change may have to be accepted when working on an individual group level, while the same aspects may well be subject to improvement when working on a higher level within the organization.

Textbox 9.2: Note

Note: Not each of the twenty dimensions will necessarily have to be worked with in every VPI process. Some dimensions may be given and not available for leverage, or they may just not be on the group's or organization's current agenda. This is another pragmatic feature of the pick-and-choose VPI approach. Interventions can be designed and executed precisely according to specific group needs and to balance other dimensions. VPI's efficiency is likely to save a customer precious time and money spent on long and less-structured diagnostic processes and uses the existing energy of the group and organization efficiently.

Team/Group/Network Development

Usually, when working with a leader and her group, the group members and their geographical distribution will be given and can't be changed.

Elements like the scope of competences and the social capital present in a group as well as the time zones determining the specific amount of Work Schedule Overlap are thus set. The same applies to the degree to which a group and its leader have Access to Information and Power within headquarters or other centres of power.

Moreover, when mandated "only" for group development, one will have to work with the given workflow systems and IT tools for communication and collaboration regardless of their suitability. The degree of management attention and the corresponding project priority within an organization's project portfolio can seldom be influenced once a project has started.

> ➤ When working with a virtual group, we often start by identifying fundamental differences in perception among group members. This is a good way to initiate a dialogue about how and why their perceptions differ.

> ➤ Limitations to what can be changed that arise from the specific organizational context need to be accepted and other levers need to be found to improve overall performance and provide a counterbalance for the other "missing" dimensions.

> ➤ At the beginning of a VPI process, it is common for a group to focus on what doesn't work rather than on what does. By guiding the group's attention to its strengths, VPI can change that perspective and help to establish a strengths-based view.

> ➤ The goal is always that all group members arrive at a shared perception of the 20 dimensions by fine-tuning them through dialogue to create a joint tune.

The VPA can be executed at different points in a VPI process:

- **At the beginning**: to determine the success factors for a virtual group and start out with the right focus.

- **During the process**: to identify improvement needs and design the corresponding improvement measures, or to measure progress, in an already-established team/group/network.

- **At the end**: as a tool to extract lessons learned and good practices for the benefit of future virtual groups.

Organization Development

When working with top management, the organizational aspects that may limit the scope of group development may now be available for analysis and subject to deliberate change.

> ➢ A consulting process on this organizational level may, for example, result in a management decision to introduce new tools for global cooperation or to promote the creation of a (perhaps additional) set of global "netiquette" guidelines. In consequence, individual groups can save a lot of precious problem-solving time by adapting revised netiquette guidelines.

> ➢ Management may also decide to implement new guidelines concerning work-place flexibility in order to enable group members to work where they feel most comfortable and productive. Likewise, geographical distribution of group members may be revised to allow for greater proximity to foreign customers. In both cases, productivity can rise significantly.

In sum, VPI processes are customized to the individual setting and can have very different designs and contents depending on the specific client situation and the resulting contract.

In the following chapter, we present four case studies to demonstrate what different VPI processes can look like.

CHAPTER TEN

Case Studies

10.1 Case Study 1: Improving Cooperation and Communication in a Global Team through a Four-step Program for Virtual Team Development at eBay

10.2 Case Study 2: Improving the Virtual Communication of a Global IT-management Group: the Importance of Process Quality

10.3 Case Study 3: Creating a Meeting Culture for a Global Automotive Supplier

10.4 Case Study 4: Creating an Online Community within RWE

In this final chapter, we present four case studies. Each of them shows how a Virtual Performance Improvement (VPI) process can be designed and executed. Since every group will produce a different "tune" based on individual perceptions of the Virtual Performance Assessment (VPA) categories, each VPI process, including the creation of the global cooperation space (the Purple Space), is tailored to the group's needs and therefore different. The following four case studies reflect this.

The first case study portrays a successful and comprehensive training of a global group within eBay. Here, we show in great detail what the different elements of a VPI process can look like, including material created for and with participants.

Case Study 2 traces a VPI process that is similar to the eBay one but smaller in scope. The crucial information here is the critical self-reflection of the VPA consultant, who designed and executed the workshop, on the importance of process quality.

Case studies 3 and 4 are two shorter studies of VPI processes that were designed to help clients build a Purple Space in two different areas relevant to virtual collaboration: creating a meeting culture and building business community.

10.1 Case Study 1: Improving Cooperation and Communication in a Global Team through a Four-step Program for Virtual Team Development at eBay

Background

One of our clients is a global group in the online market sector within eBay. The core of the client team that initiated the consulting contract is based in the UK and responsible for all European dependencies. The head office is located in the USA.

While cooperation and communication between the UK and the US groups worked well on an individual level, they were impeded on the group level. The UK group complained that their colleagues in the US were not taking into account the needs and concerns of the Europeans enough, planning and implementing rollouts solely from a US perspective.

We were asked to work with the UK and US groups to improve their cooperation and communication.

Structural Challenges

One of the structural challenges resulted from the core team being located in the UK, while team partners are dispersed in the US and in Germany. They formally belong to the team but are not placed under the direct team leadership. With a core team at the centre, the group is thus structured like a matrix or a network.

The UK group is further dealing with the fact that the US partners are located closer to the power centre of the organization, and thus to its decision makers and core processes. At the same time, however, they are only more or less loosely attached to the global team. In consequence, the UK group has sometimes felt left alone and neglected regarding the transparency of central decisions and the implementation of new processes. They felt that the needs of the European market were not properly respected by US headquarters. Interestingly, it later turned out that the German representative had the same reservations about the European head office in the UK: the team was in "ignoring mode". This illustrates an important generic feature of the client's organizational system.

The Four-step Program for Virtual Team Development

We developed and implemented a four-step program that respected the structural challenge of our main client (the core team of the global network) being located in the UK. That way, the intervention has empowered the core team by assigning it the role of pacemaker within the network, defining the global team's heartbeat.

The four-step program is an example of what a customized Virtual Performance Improvement process can be like. It consists of one face-to-face and three virtual elements.

Figure 10.1: 4-Step Program for Virtual Team Development

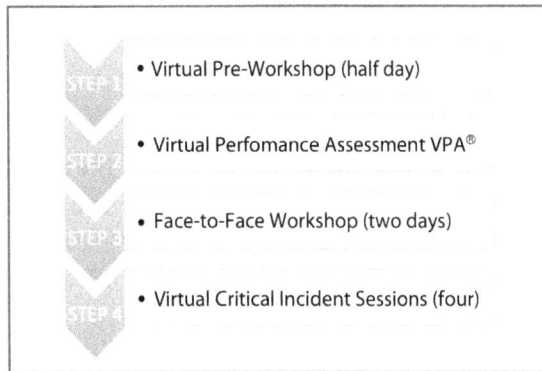

STEP 1 • Virtual Pre-Workshop (half day)

STEP 2 • Virtual Perfomance Assessment VPA®

STEP 3 • Face-to-Face Workshop (two days)

STEP 4 • Virtual Critical Incident Sessions (four)

Step 1: Virtual Pre-workshop (half day)

In a first step, we engaged the UK group in a half-day virtual training session on intercultural aspects of teamwork. The purpose of this event was twofold. First, participants and coaches got to know each other. Second, awareness of US working and communicating styles was enhanced and ways to better transport the UK team's messages to improve the virtual interaction with US headquarters were identified.

The group was together in one room in the UK. The coaches connected with them from two different places in Germany via phone and Skype conferencing. A presentation was shared and meeting minutes were taken in a chat room during the event.

Exhibit 10.1: Workshop Agenda

Workshop Agenda

09:30 – 09:35	Checking in / Agenda
09:35 – 09:45	Getting to know each other
09:45 – 09:50	The four steps / Aim for today
09:50 – 10:10	Define virtual key players
10:10 – 10:30	Input on virtual closeness
10:30 – 10:45	Break
10:45 – 11:15	The "US" way of communicating and working
11:15 – 11:45	Text based communication: Preparing the US trip
11:45 – 12:00	Break
12:00 – 12:10	Text-based communication: Preparing the US trip (cont.)
12:10 – 12:15	Let us change perspectives
12:15 – 12:45	Presentation and discussion
12:45 – 13:00	Feedback and outlook

Answers to the question, **"What works and what are our challenges in the collaboration with the US colleagues?"** included, for example:

- Direct communication works

- Following up in writing works

- Boarding negative feedback doesn't really work

- They are not aware of our context.

Statements on **"learning points from the virtual session"** included, for example:

- Remember to talk about the future effect of a change

- Focus on the similarities between *us* and *them*

- Remember to look at things from their perspective and at their perception of the project timing.

Step 2: Virtual Performance Assessment (VPA)

Next, we conducted a Virtual Performance Assessment that provided us with insights into the virtual-performance status of the global team, of the UK group, and of the US group. Most network/core-team members completed the questionnaire. Based on the survey results, we designed the Step 3 face-to-face workshop.

We provided our customer with the following accumulated survey results:

- Results of their US partners

- Results of the European team members and partners

- Results of the whole team

- Results of the individual assessments of those team members who filled in the questionnaire (these results were handed out only to those who owned the corresponding questionnaire).

This enabled us to compare the results with a view to the different perceptions on both sides of the US–UK interface, highlighting those areas where they agreed or disagreed and displaying the individual deviations from the mean values.

Based on these results and together with the client group, we designed a customized face-to-face workshop to address the most problematic topics ("hot spots") within the global team. The VPA results thus offered a new and more solid base for our communication and intervention with the members.

Figure 10.2: Selected Results of the Virtual Performance Assessment of the Global Team

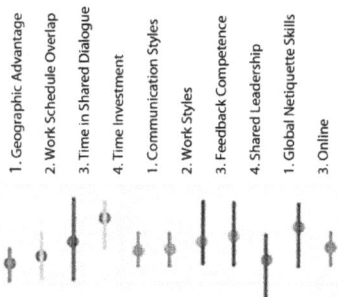

The vertical lines depict the variation of perspectives within the team:

- Red: largest variations

- Orange: significant variations

- Green: similar perspectives.

Figure 10.3: Selected Results of the Virtual Performance Assessment of the UK Group

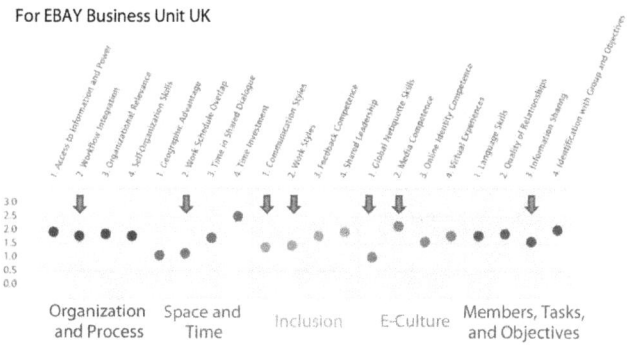

For EBAY Business Unit UK

| Organization and Process | Space and Time | Inclusion | E-Culture | Members, Tasks, and Objectives |

(The arrows indicate different values compared to the US group.)

Step 3: Face-to-face Workshop (two days)

The VPA results provided an enhanced ground for our communication with the workshop participants. We structured the workshop around comparing the assessment results from three different perspectives: the UK group's results, the US group's results, and the overall global group results, reflecting the often very different perceptions of both groups.

Exhibit 10.2: Workshop Agenda (Step 3)

Workshop Agenda (Step 3)

Day 1

- Overview of the four steps
- Introduction of the two facilitators
- Individual reflection of current work situation and workshop expectations; status report (whole group)
- Consolidation: lessons learned from virtual workshop and topics for the workshop
- Collaboration simulation: Broken Squares
- Input on collaboration / diversity and performance of a team -> fake tolerance / friendly avoidance, different modes of reaction if voicing does not take place -> voicing as a key method
- Creating purple culture: defining global feedback culture / feedback competence:
  - Input on the three factors of response cultures: driver, process, setting while explaining the task
  - Effort to harvest shared behaviours
- Speed Input on virtual closeness and five categories
- Interpretation of VPA questionnaire in the context of US–UK interface (work in tandems):
  - Presentation of overall results: Orientation
  - Lessons learned and topics for the workshop → Content container
  - Go for the weakest point and try to identify ways to turn it into a strength: in this case, geographic advantage (promote your site: why is it great that you are where you are)
- Strengths of the team
- Feedback and wishes (closing)

Day 2

- Introduction to the agenda
- Global Netiquette:
  - Online Identity
  - Which media for which purpose?
  - Group work: optimization of media usage (pick your relevant media and/or the communication situations)
- Presentation/discussion
- Simulation: "Mouse Face" and working styles / Lewis model
- U-Game: learning – plug and play process (including the heartbeat): placing it, starting it, running it, closing it (two different settings)
  - Debriefing: learning points

Transfer Management

- Think of an initiative/learning you would like to spread in your setting (brainstorming, decision making, etc.)
- Work on the different topics combined with inputs on:
  - Shared Leadership
  - Time in shared dialogue / heartbeat of a team
  - Online Identity
  - Global Netiquette skills
- What is the initiative?
  - How can the topic be introduced?
  - How can the topic be monitored?
- Planning of next steps (virtual critical-incidents meetings) and feedback

Day 1

The workshop content was based on what the VPA results showed about group members' perceptions of their virtual collaboration. After an initial reflection on the previous virtual training (Step 1), we concentrated on the details of the two groups' cooperation and communication. Employing a method mix of input presentations, team exercises, and discussions, the workshop was highly participative and practical.

We started with collecting desired workshop outcomes.

Exhibit 10.3: Outcomes

- Global planning → How to get initiatives better across?
- Align our languages together → getting away from negative pictures
- Taking advantage of precious face-to-face time
- Transparency
- Common understanding → closer working relations
- Where we are coming from → context of teams
- Getting away from frustrating each other
- Get closed to the team
- Prioritization
- Taking the opportunity to exchange experiences with U.S. colleagues → Shared understanding
- Understanding people's motivation
- Understanding how to explain things better to others

Based on those outcome expectations, we were able to define jointly with the workshop participants the objectives and areas of improvement to be addressed during the workshop. We stored all concerns in a content container.

Exhibit 10.4: Content Container

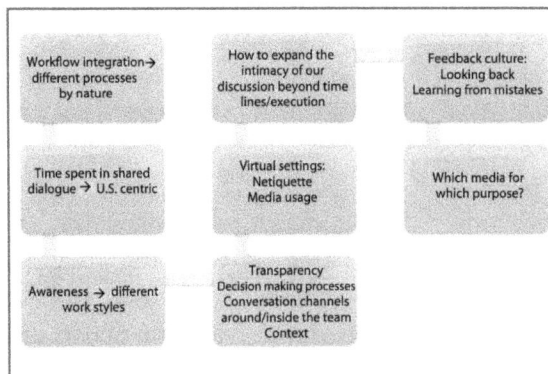

Using the "Broken Squares" exercise (a cooperation simulation), participants reflected on the basic duality that exists in most organizational settings: Us and Them. Group dynamics are often based on this division and, in the absence of conscious reflection, groups cooperate but do not collaborate. And usually, they don't communicate enough. The ensuing feeling of being disconnected makes Virtual Closeness very difficult to build. It is sometimes important to deconstruct local success in favour of global success.

We therefore focused on introducing and practising how to develop a feedback culture. The central aspect of feedback is regular, fearless, and respectful *voicing* of concerns, criticism, recognition and so forth. To emphasize the importance of this particular type of communication, we used an exercise to show different reactions in situations in which people don't speak openly about their perceptions (see also the Nine Levels of Not Voicing in Section 2.3). The exercise shows how important a voicing culture is and how fake tolerance and friendly avoidance sabotage cooperation.

We dedicated the second half of the first day to working through the VPA outputs, starting with the overall results of the entire group. Since the VPA is taken individually, everyone who answered the survey sees her or his particular results upon completing it. The administrators also see the individual results and – most importantly for team development – their synthesis in the group output. Presented with their respective individual results and those of the group, and thus able to compare the two, the participants broke into small voicing groups of two or three and shared why they perceive certain aspects of their group's virtual performance differently or similarly relative to the group average. This exercise helped the group to familiarize itself further with VPA and gave them a chance to practise voicing their perceptions.

Exhibit 10.5: Reflecting VPA Results

> ✓ Share your observations in groups of 4. Where does your individual assessment differ significantly from the group average?
>
> ✓ Challenge each other: How come you assesssed those dimensions the way you did?
>
> --> Voice it in the subsequent plenary session.

Moving on to comparing the results of the UK and the US groups, one rather striking assessment output revealed that neither subgroup perceived their geographical locations as advantageous for collaboration. To promote their respective sites, the group members explored the hidden benefits of their locations and "sold" them to their colleagues.

After an intensive day of working through the challenges of virtual collaboration, we ended by exploring and appreciating the strengths of the team to finish with a sense of balance.

Exhibit 10.6: Strengths of the team

- Diversity
- Get along quite well / good atmosphere
- Genuinely follow the same goals / objectives
- Passionate team
- We have the right resources
- Desire to work better together
- Mutual respect for each other / respecting expertise
- If necessary we invest a lot of time
- Knowing whom to contact
- Low complexity
- Willingness to share information
- Local market knowledge and diversity of thought
- Time difference = thinking time

Through asking "What makes our location interesting for colleagues in other locations? What is attractive about our location?" participants could appreciate, for example, the immense benefit of the US team being located in Silicon Valley. On the other hand, reflecting on the unique culture of that location, the US participants better understood that a general global rollout is not effective and needs to be adapted to local circumstances.

Day 2

The second day was dedicated to discussing the group's E-Culture and Work Styles.

An interesting VPA finding about this high-tech group was that, in spite of the very high Media Competence of all the participants, the levels of Global Netiquette Skills differed significantly among them. Moreover, Online Identity skills proved to be relatively underdeveloped. We therefore presented an input on Global Netiquette Skills and Online Identity skills.

The participants then worked to identify the right media mix to cope with the previously identified communications difficulties between the

US and UK groups. The following image shows an example of how the team thought about changing its approach to brainstorming sessions after our input presentation, "Which media for which purpose?"

Exhibit 10.7: Brainstorming: Media Mix

Anonymous confidence/honest	• F2F/non-anonymous
Problem No anonymous media available	• Need a way to reassure participant on rules of the brainstorming session
Solution 1. IT to set up anonymous internal chat/forum/blog/Wiki 2. Real time: Link/Skype/Adobe Connect 3. Set up over a couple of days gives more time for clear thinking and more ideas 4. Ideas collected and grouped, and voted for anonymously	• Multi-channel media

We completed the training with an input on Work Styles, followed by a virtual simulation exercise on remote leadership called the "U-Game". By exploring lessons learned, particularly on how to place, start, run and close a topic, the group developed shared norms to include the different Work Styles of its members. These interventions helped to reduce the existing complexity and shape the group's Purple Space. The group negotiated and adapted joint media usage and shared Work Styles.

Step 4: Virtual Critical-incident Sessions (four sessions)

The last phase of the program consisted of four virtual sessions. Each was prepared and led by a different group member who presented a critical incident from the global group's work, which was then discussed among the participants. Participants came from both the US and the UK group and, in the case of the latter, from different locations across Europe. Eight different group members and two external moderators participated in every session.

The sessions were structured voicing exercises. Discussing critical incidents, the participants practised voicing as well as the giving and receiving of feedback by finding solutions for the respective issue together. In so doing, the group developed a culture of Shared Leadership.

We asked the US-based group to present the first critical incident. Given that, often, only its own work issues are of interest to a team, group, or network and that such egotism was at the centre of the initial complaint by the UK team about their US counterparts, we wanted to give the UK people a chance to reflect on their own perception. By asking the US group to lead the first meeting, the UK colleagues quickly became conscious of the impulse to ignore the other's problem and concentrate on one's own instead. By reflecting this within the group, a shared responsibility for critical incidents concerning the entire group emerged and acts of Shared Leadership have since been initiated by both sides.

Results

The group members have shared the following improvements resulting from the four-step program:

- ✓ More access to detailed information

- ✓ Monthly meetings

- ✓ Socially better chatting (private)

- ✓ Team's heartbeat improved

- ✓ Several joint Wikis have been established, emails are being used less

- ✓ Much better communication

- ✓ No more finger pointing but finding of common solutions

- ✓ More informal ways to catch up

- ✓ Wider sense of what is going on

- ✓ UK: team now think about US first

- ✓ US: step away from "US first and then the others will surely love it" towards "get others' input right away"

✓ All are now mindful of the communication gap; it is no longer assumed that all have the same information

✓ More use is made of synchronous meeting technology instead of emails

✓ Deeper-going professional discussions (for example, discussing pros and cons).

Textbox 10.1: Key Takeaways

The advantage of hearing both sides

- builds trust and clears up confusion
- through voicing (using the team clock gives everyone a voice)

Lessons Learned: Areas of Improvement

The difficulties encountered during the four-step program fall into two categories: technological issues and organizational reach.

Technology

The technological problems we faced are typical for virtual cooperation. Three issues surfaced in particular:

1. The choice of communication tools was limited by the fact that the group had to use the company's software

2. The UK and US groups had different routines and preferences about which tools they use for virtual collaboration

3. The two groups had difficulty agreeing on joint virtual communication tools.

Organizational Reach

Two aspects were critical here. First, the UK team didn't consider inviting their US colleagues initially because of a feeling that the latter wouldn't join. When the external facilitators suggested giving it a try nonetheless, the group decided to invite their US co-workers to join the face-to-face workshop. While only three people from the US did join, the UK team was very happy to have them. They realized that it would have been good to invite the US colleagues to participate in the process from the beginning.

Second, this need to get more group members involved in the joint process points to the larger systemic need of increased buy-in, both from group members and from management. Organizational change crucially depends on leadership support in order to have ripple effects on the whole organization.

Motivated by their positive experience, the group is considering lobbying with senior management for an organization-wide process to improve virtual collaboration, presenting their four-step process as a successful pilot. They plan to articulate clearly why Virtual Performance Improvement is needed.

Lessons Learned from the VPI Point of View

- The process would have benefitted from a stronger involvement of the US team during the pre-phase of the program, especially on a higher hierarchical level.

- We designed the virtual workshop (Step 1) with a focus on the European participants, thereby getting the perspective of just one part of the group. However, this first phase can also be implemented with both parts of a group, in which case the contents need to be adapted accordingly.

- Virtual follow-up approaches could be redesigned to have two or three critical-incidents sessions with all group members and a joint closing session to discuss next steps without the external facilitators.

- At some point further into the process, ask participants to fill in the VPA questionnaire again to monitor the changing group "tune".

10.2 Case Study 2: Improving the Virtual Communication of a Global IT-management Group: the Importance of Process Quality

Background

A global company in the packaging industry wanted to use a face-to-face meeting, taking place in Northern Europe, of their global IT management group to reflect upon their intercultural and virtual communication practices, and to use their learning to develop good practice. The intention was to begin with this group of learners in order subsequently to improve the overall level of virtual performance in all company project teams that collaborate internationally.

Workshop Design

Developed in partnership between an external consultant, the client sponsor and the group leader, a two-day workshop was outlined for the benefit of the IT management group. As a first step, all 14 participants from 10 different countries spread across the globe – from New Zealand to Brazil, Thailand to Russia – were invited to fill out a Virtual Performance Assessment (VPA) questionnaire to assess their level of closeness in group collaboration. Some of the group members had already built a high degree of social capital (*Virtual Experiences*) over the several years of their collaboration, while others were fairly new to the group. Two members had in fact never met face-to-face with any of the others, while all of them knew the leader from face-to-face settings in their respective home locations.

VPA Results: Hot Spots for VPI

The evaluation of the scores showed a lot of medium range in the dimensions, with a few giving impulses to examine them more closely. While the dimensions of *Time Investment* and *Media Competence* were strongly developed, *Global Netiquette Skills* was a dimension that invited a closer look. It was ranked lowest (please recall that "low" in the context of VPA does not mean "negative"). A little less pronounced, but also inviting consideration, were the dimensions of *Geographic Advantage, Work Schedule Overlap, Communication Styles, Work Styles, Feedback Competence*, and *Shared Leadership*.

A still more conclusive picture was offered by the spread-evaluation that shows the range between the scores by the participants. While *Media Competence* was overall ranked rather highly, the spread was significant and was a strong indication that team members had very diverse views on how well the team was using the collaboration media at its disposal. Spreads that also invited a closer examination of the differences that became visible amongst the team members included *Geographic Advantage, Time in Shared Dialogue*, and *Feedback Competence*. Taking a look at the individual scores, it became clear that some of the spreads' diverse positions could be traced to different cultural clusters, especially to team members in Asian and European cultures.

Specific Additional Training Needs: Intercultural and Virtual Communication

After discussing the scores with the team leader and helping him to understand the results, the workshop design needed to take into account that while a few of the European members had taken part in an intercultural competence development training before, the vast majority of the members lacked the knowledge and vocabulary to describe their challenges in intercultural contexts adequately. The same was true for the practice of virtual communication, for which the group had never received any training. It thus was clear from the start that whatever areas the VPA offered as entry points into the performance improvement process of the team, it would need to be amended by inputs and learning in the areas of virtual and intercultural communication – and, potentially also in project management and organizational contexts.

Case-specific Challenge: Communication between Leader and Consultant

The consultant asked the team leader to identify a maximum of three areas corresponding to VPA dimensions on which the workshop would focus. While the team leader formally agreed on the three dimensions of *Global Netiquette Skills*, *Geographic Advantage* and *Communication Styles*, he asked whether *Media Competence* (with *Global Netiquette Skills*), *Work Schedule Overlap* (with *Geographic Advantage*), and *Work Styles* and *Feedback Competence* (with *Communication Styles*) might also be integrated into the workshop.

Here, the consultant failed to close a gap in communication that later grew to much larger proportions. While he stated that these dimensions could not be collapsed and that working on one dimension alone might take from half a day up to one full day to achieve satisfactory results for the group, he nevertheless offered to mention some of the aspects contained in the related dimensions.

Another missed opportunity by the consultant was not establishing agreement with the group leader on how decision-making processes should be designed. Should the team make suggestions to the leader? Or did the leader want to invite open decision-making processes, potentially in consensus? According to the leader, "We are practising an open leadership culture and are mature enough to discuss decisions openly".

Workshop Content

DAY 1 – Morning

- Introduction to the challenges of diversity in virtual teams: simulation and input

- Getting to know a few "intercultural basics" in communication (including the cultural dimension of Hierarchy and Egalitarianism and ideas around conflict management, as well as exercises with critical incidents and group examples)

- Introduction to the concept of "Virtual Closeness" (including an exercise, and subsequent participant input and discussion)

- Analyzing and interpreting the VPA values of the team (in the form of subgroup and plenary discussion)

- Agreeing on a course for the remainder of the day (in the form of subgroup and plenary discussion).

DAY 1 – Afternoon

Work on initial "hot spots" of the group: *Communication Styles* and *Work Styles*

Participants first worked for 10 minutes by themselves, then formed subgroups as diverse as possible. The guiding questions for subgroup discussion were:

- Three aspects that you would like to see changed in the work and/or communication styles detectable in the team;

- Three aspects in your own work and/or communication style that would be negotiable; and

- Three aspects that seem impossible for you to change.

Participants first answered these questions individually, then presented and discussed their ideas within their subgroup, receiving feedback from the other members about their perspectives. Thus a rich texture of conversation was opened by participants on perceptions about the diversity in the group. Subgroup conversations were further enriched by a whole-group discussion ("Marketplace") where each subgroup reported three highlights from their discussion.

Clustering of topics deriving from *Communication Styles* and *Work Styles*

From here, the group identified overarching patterns emerging from their responses and discussed which of these they would later want to integrate into the group's netiquette, including:

- Organizing into learning tandems, and identifying group members' needs to which flexible/adaptive behaviour seemed possible

- Agreeing on a feedback format for the tandems on how, and how often, to coach both individual group members and the whole group in possible behavioural adaptations to work and communication styles.

DAY 2 – Morning

Work on *Feedback Competence*

As a first point in the morning, the group dealt with the Virtual Performance Assessment (VPA) dimension of *Feedback Competence*. Activities included the following:

- Exercise in "Feedback Traffic Light" and the importance of "voicing" in high-performance, international groups

- Discussion of feedback dimensions within international contexts (specifically referring to the InterPersonal Feedback Profiler*, a new model development from original research)

- Analysis of the current feedback practice in the group using the InterPersonal Feedback Profiler model (in the form of subgroup work and presentations)

- Application: agreement on the five most important aspects of feedback in the group (in the form of subgroups and plenary discussions)

- Identification of "Feedback Champions" to monitor the practice within the group (informal setting).

Work on *Media Competence*

The group then dealt with the VPA dimension *Media Competence*, which had shown a great discrepancy in the score. In response, the

---

*   If you're interested in more details about the InterPersonal Feedback Profiler and the original research that has informed it, kindly contact info@intercultures.de.

following exercise was used:

- "Which media for which purpose?" This exercise compares the diverse practices of media employment within the team and shows which media might be best used for which purpose, taking special cultural practices into account. It is a suitable preparation for negotiating team netiquette, which followed in the afternoon.

DAY 2 – Afternoon

Work on *Global Netiquette Skills* and dealing with process and leadership related conflict

Aiming at integrating the intercultural knowledge and the differences in *Work* and *Communication Styles*, the group's desired feedback practice and the newly acquired *Media Competence*, developing its *Global Netiquette Skills* was planned as a closing highlight for the workshop.

It took a large part of the afternoon to come up with very concrete suggestions. When the results were presented by subgroups in the whole-group plenary discussion, it became evident that the group had no decision-making mandate. Even though the leader had stated that decisions could be taken in the plenary, he absolutely rejected some suggestions (e.g. local team leaders to be cc'd when emailing Asian-based colleagues) as they did not, in his perspective, reflect the kind of leadership he wanted in the group. The lack of authentic alignment between leader and consultant before the workshop became visible. Remember: when the topic of an agreement process was previously and briefly approached by the consultant, the group leader's answer was that, "We are practising an open leadership culture and are mature enough to discuss decisions openly".

Needless to say, the leader's intervention not only nearly stopped discussion, but seriously endangered the motivation for any agreement about company netiquette. At the next workshop break, the consultant discussed the potentially damaging nature of the intervention to the motivation of the group with the leader and their next possible steps.

It was agreed that the last point of the agenda, *Geographic Advantage*, and the "how-to" of implementing netiquette would be tasked to specific task groups.

Going Forward

It was decided that, for the task group that dealt with *Geographic Advantage*, members located in a different location would co-host the next synchronous virtual meeting. They would take five minutes to introduce the value that their specific geographic location adds to the whole group. The task group that dealt with *Netiquette Skills* would monitor only those points that were seen as non-critical by the group and the leader, thus leading to a light, reduced version of a shared netiquette – which can be practical, but also frustrating in practice.

Lessons Learned

In summary, the analysis made through the Virtual Performance Assessment (VPA) with the global IT-management group intervention helped to visualize and structure the corresponding workshop in a very practical manner. Increased success could have been achieved with a previously discussed and agreed-upon alignment between the leader and the consultant about how decisions would be made during the workshop.

Two strong learning points emerging from this case study are:

➢ As a VPA consultant, make sure you have an authentic agreement on how a decision-making process will proceed in a workshop based on VPA dimensions; and,

➢ As always, less is more. Avoid trying to squeeze in too many "hot spots" into a workshop, but aim for a few areas, or even just one, and give room for client partners to develop and come to a solid state that is attractive enough for participants to implement in their professional practice.

10.3 Case Study 3: Creating a Meeting Culture for a Global Automotive Supplier

Background

A global automotive supplier wants to create a meeting culture shared by its European locations and subsequently by all locations globally. This is a first and major step towards creating a global Purple Space in a participatory way by involving employees. It flows from the realization that meetings tend to be part of the problem rather than the solution. When meetings don't have a clear purpose and a shared culture, they tend to be neither efficient nor productive and turn into a waste of time for many members. Different people tend to have different ideas and expectations around the purpose and content of meetings and when these are not met, often feel annoyed and unmotivated.

Our client has decided to counter these tendencies by developing a Purple Space around meetings. The aim is to increase meeting efficiency, employee satisfaction, and cost saving.

Approach

In a pilot workshop we facilitated, members from all hierarchical levels and different national cultures defined a general framework for a meeting culture including topics like:

- What constitutes a meeting in our company?

- What are vital questions around meetings that have to be answered either in a globally standardized way or in a locally adapted version?

- Which IT structure could support the process of establishing a new meeting culture?

In a next step, we facilitated two-day training workshops throughout the company. These consisted of two elements:

- Training related to intercultural aspects of meeting culture, improving the efficiency of virtual meetings, and voicing critical issues around meeting culture in order to initiate continuous improvement processes etc.

- Workshop/organization development such as: analyzing the different meeting types members experience in their daily work; collecting feedback on the results from the pilot workshop; and asking participants to create a list of meeting guidelines.

In an upcoming final step, it is envisioned that the data gathered during the workshops will be consolidated, approved by the company, communicated top down throughout the company, and backed up by relevant IT systems. The benefit of the described approach is that at the time of implementation, employees and leaders will already be trained to make efficient use of the new, shared guidelines.

Overcoming Challenges by "Hunting for the No"

As can be expected, the process described above often called for finding consensus on the specifics of building a global approach to meetings within a multicultural and diverse group.

Consider the following example that illustrates the process of "Hunting for the No" described in Chapter Seven (pages 183–7).

Workshop participants identified meeting types in need of global guidelines. Examples included customer/supplier meetings and management review meetings. All participants agreed that these meeting types ought to be improved by implementing global guide-lines. While it would have been easy to finalize the process by producing a majority vote (Who is in favor of this decision?), we opted for a different approach: "hunting for the no".

We started to "hunt for the no" with respect to the identified list of meeting types by asking each participant individually about their gut feeling: should this list be submitted for board approval to be imple-mented throughout the company? We elicited one weak signal and one answer that indicated a "No":

➢ "No": "There are many more meeting types on the list. Shouldn't all of them be ruled by global guidelines? If guidelines are set only for selected meeting types, people might find excuses for avoiding them. For example, an excuse could be that a meeting isn't considered important enough to create an agenda, etc. I think we are going in the wrong direction."

➢ Weak signal: "I think the principles are okay but I'm afraid the board will be overshooting. This has happened in similar cases in the past when we ended up with a very rigid and inflexible system of norms and regulations, foreclosing the implementation of a new meeting culture."

Based on their statements we asked the two participants "What in the current and future approach should be changed, and how, to make you more comfortable with taking the decision?"

The participant who expressed the "No" suggested the creation of "a subset of the guiding principles to be applied to all meetings organization wide." The other participant mentioned some ideas that might help to prevent a possible "overshooting" by the board.

Based on this, we formulated a decision package with which all participants agreed and reached a consensus on the next steps.

10.4 Case Study 4: Creating an Online Community within RWE

Background and Challenges

RWE, a global energy provider, wanted to create a purple interaction space by setting up a web-based community for controllers.

The community is supported by an intranet platform. Its main purpose is to support the improvement of controllers' performance by helping to:

• Improve their information exchange

- Enlarge the distance of the reach of their communication

- Support their collaboration at a distance

- Identify good practice and spread it within the community

- Contribute to the development of the organizational culture through increased knowledge exchange and heightened inter-action across hierarchies.

The community's identity is characterized by the following features:

- Participation is voluntary

- The community has a logo and an individual name

- It is a closed group of 1,000 controllers, allowing temporary access only to invited external experts and guests in the context of dedicated online/f2f events

- It focuses on the cognitive and knowledge sharing level more than on the relationship level.

Before creating the new online community, controllers (beneath the level of departmental heads) had only a few steered interactions/meetings that offered sufficient opportunities for networking and good-practice exchange.

Approach

By introducing regular synchronous and asynchronous online events such as:

- Broadcasts

- Workshops

- Blogs

- Networking serious games

the organization envisions significant improvements to the existing community.

In a two-day workshop on "Global Cooperation and Virtual Performance Improvement", three small groups of controllers worked on developing ideas for establishing a globally shared collaboration (purple) space. The purpose of this Purple Space is to create a systematic and professional approach to coping with intercultural differences in communication and behaviour, especially in meetings.

Their main strategies to shape the Purple Space and reduce complexity include:

➢ Increasing awareness of intercultural issues in an appreciative way

➢ Defining a (non-negotiable) set of successful global cooperation behaviours by collecting good practice from the different member cultures in order to improve cooperation across cultures and to avoid "show stoppers"

➢ Creating a web-based toolbox to improve voicing and facilitating skills within the community.

References

Anderson, T., L. Rourke, R. Garrison, and W. Archer (2001) Assessing Teaching Presence in a Computer Conferencing Context. *Journal of Asynchronous Learning Networks* 5(2), 1–17

Caulat, Ghislaine (2012) *Virtual Leadership: Learning to Lead Differently.* Faringdon: Libri

Cummings, J., and Martine Haas (2012) So Many Teams, So Little Time: Time Allocation Matters in Geographically Dispersed Teams. *Journal of Organizational Behavior* (33) 316

DiStefano, Joseph J., and Martha L. Maznevski (2000) Creating Value with Diverse Teams in Global Management. *Organizational Dynamics* Vol. 29, No. 1, 45–63

Ferrazzi, Keith (2012) Virtual Teams Can Outperform Traditional Teams. *Harvard Business Review* Blog, 03/2012

Forchhammer, Lorenz (2012) Der virtuelle Chef. *Personalwissenschaft* (8) 2012, 58–9

Garrison, D.R., Terry Anderson, and W. Archer (2000) Critical Inquiry in a Text-Based Environment: Computer Conferencing in Higher Education. *The Internet and Higher Education* 2 (2–3), 1–19

Garrison, D.R., and Terry Anderson (2003) *E-Learning in the 21st Century: A Framework for Research and Practice.* RoutledgeFalmer: London

Kostner, Jaclyn (1996) *Virtual Leadership: Secrets from the Round Table for the Multi-Site Manager.* Grand Central Publishing

Kotter, John (2001) What Leaders Really Do. *Harvard Business Review*

Lipnack, Jessica, and Jeffrey Stamps (2000) *Virtual Teams: People Working Across Boundaries with Technology.* John Wiley & Sons

Lojeski, Karen Sobel, and Richard R. Reilly (2008) *Uniting the Virtual Workforce: Transforming Leadership and Innovation in the Globally Integrated Enterprise.* John Wiley & Sons

Majchrzak, Ann, Arvind Malhotra, Jeffrey Stamps, and Jessica Lipnack (2004) Can Absence Make a Team Grow Stronger? *Harvard Business Review* 82 (5)

Maznevski, Martha L., and Katherine M. Chudoba (2000) Bridging Space Over Time: Global Virtual Team Dynamics and Effectiveness. *Organization Science* 11 (5)

Maznevski, Martha L., Sue Canney, and Karsten Jonsen (2006) Creating Effective Virtual Teams: Getting Off the Ground. *Tomorrow's Challenges*, November 2006

Moxley, R.S. (2000) *Leadership and Spirit.* Jossey-Bass

Nandhakumar, Joe, and Richard Baskerville (2001) Trusting Online: Nurturing Trust in Virtual Teams. Paper presented at the 9th European Conference in Information Systems on Global Co-operation in the New Millennium

Nemerowicz, G., and E. Rosi (1997) *Education for Leadership and Social Responsibility.* Falmer Press

Nemiro, Jill (1997) *Creativity in Virtual Teams: Key Components for Success.* Jossey-Bass/Pfeiffer

Nemiro, Jill (2004) *The Collaborative Work Systems Fieldbook: Strategies, Tools, and Techniques.* Jossey-Bass/Pfeiffer

Rath, Tom, and Barry Conchie (2009) *Strengths Based Leadership: Great Leaders, Teams, and Why People Follow.* Gallup Press

Salmon, Gilly (2004) *E-Moderating: The Key to Online Teaching and Learning.* Routledge

Schütze, Dorothea, and Marcus Hildebrandt (2006) Demokratische Schulentwicklung: Partizipations- und Aushandlungsansätze im Berliner BLK-Vorhaben „Demokratie lernen und leben". RAA Berlin

Schweizer, K., M. Pächter, and B. Weidenmann (2002) Learning in

Segalla, Michael and Karl Sandner (2010) Die globale Telefonkonferenz. *Harvard Business Manager* November 2010.

Synchronous and Asynchronous Virtual Teams. Paper presented at the EARLI SIG 6

Siebdrat, Frank, Martin Hoegl, and Holger Ernst (2009) How to Manage Virtual Teams. *MIT Sloan Management Review* 50 (4)

Ulrich, Susanne (2005) Achtung (+) Toleranz: Wege demokratischer Konfliktregelung. Praxishandbuch für die politische Bildung. Gütersloh

Wyatt, David K. (2003) *Thailand – A Short History.* Yale University Press

Online Resources

Deep Democracy Institute: http://www.deepdemocracyinstitute.org/
deep-democracy-explained.html

IMD Tomorrow's Challenges: http://www.imd.org/research/challenges/
TC058-06.cfm

Lewis, Myrna: Inside the No, http://www.deep-democracy.net

Pateau Consultants: http://www.pateauconsultants.com/en/index.php

TMI (Too Much Information): http://boydio.wordpress.com/2011/03/08/
no-more-email-in-3-years-good-luck-with-that/

WorldWork: www.worldwork.biz

About the Authors

Dr. Marcus Hildebrandt is founder and Managing Director of learning.de and head of Virtual Performance Improvement (VPI®) at intercultures. Marcus has been working internationally as an executive coach and consultant in the fields of Personnel Development, Leadership Development, and Organization Development, and has created innovative learning and meeting formats for the past 16 years. A physicist by training, he has done pioneering work on virtual teams, and on e-coaching and e-moderation. He co-developed the Virtual Performance Assessment (VPA®) and the Interpersonal Feedback Profiler, two tools that help professionals to improve the performance of global teams, groups, and networks. Marcus can be reached at marcus.hildebrandt@learning.de.

Line Jehle is founder and Managing Director of perform-globally.com. She has been working internationally as an Executive Coach and Consultant for the past 18 years. Her professional focus is on helping organizations to improve their global performance through executive training courses and coaching. Because of her Danish heritage and time spent living and working abroad, Line has directly felt and experienced the influences of different cultures. Line co-developed the Virtual Performance Assessment (VPA®), a tool that helps professionals understand how they can improve the performance of global teams, groups, and networks. She is a member of the International Coaching Federation. Line can be reached at linejehle@perform-globally..com.

Stefan Meister is founder and Managing Director of intercultures, an international consulting and training company that helps organizations to work efficiently with global complexity. As a trainer, consultant, and coach he has worked with over 70 companies in more than 30 different countries. As most international business communication today is virtual, Stefan sees virtual performance as a key factor for future organizational success. He has co-created the Virtual Performance Assessment (VPA)® and the Interpersonal Feedback Profiler. Stefan can be reached at meister@intercultures.de.

Susanne Skoruppa works as a consultant, coach and author at the nexus of Organization Development and conflict resolution. A lawyer and organizational psychologist, she has worked for the United Nations, the World Bank and a number of national public and private organizations, and has ample experience working in and with intercultural, virtual teams and groups. Susanne has lived and worked in the U.S., several European countries and in South East Asia. She holds postgraduate degrees from the University of London and has trained in mediation and counseling. She also teaches at the Free University of Berlin. Susanne can be reached at skoruppas@gmail.com.

We invite you to join our community "Closeness at a Distance" on LinkedIn with the email address closeness@a-distance.com.